Praise for *The* ___, ___

"This book is an outstanding sequel to *The Wise Leader* and is essential reading, not only for those in leadership positions but also for anyone who truly wants to become his or her best self. The '12 Core Values' are an invaluable framework for developing skills and attributes that foster empowering relationships. The authors have drawn from the best in social, spiritual, personal, and organizational development, as well as from their own rich experiences and lifelong journeys. I am pleased and proud to recommend *The Empowering Leader*."

—**Bill Milliken**, founder of Communities in Schools;
author of *The Last Dropout* and *From the Rearview Mirror*

"Here they go again. Paul D. Houston and Stephen L. Sokolow have a track record of writing about leadership that cuts to the chaste. In *The Empowering Leader*, the two draw on experience and wisdom to reveal the heart and soul of leadership. Today's organizations are dominated by the coolness of rationality rather than the warmth of rapture, sentiment, and significance. A better path will be hewn only by leaders who are in touch with their potency and passion. Houston and Sokolow show the way. A refreshing departure from today's managerial status quo."

—**Terrence E. Deal**, author of *Leading with
Soul* and *Reframing the Path to School Leadership*

"*The Empowering Leader: 12 Core Values to Supercharge your Leadership Skills* takes us beyond their last book *The Wise Leader* into the depths of effective leadership. We learn about intention, intuition (your hidden knowledge), your higher self, openness (to expand possibilities), and much more, including two bonus gifts for going deeper—our hidden guidance system and constructive action. If you want to do the right thing and make it happen in practice, read and absorb *The Empowering Leader*. Sokolow and Houston take their years of experience and insight into the future of leadership. Here is a book that is at once inspiring and action-packed."

—**Michael Fullan**, professor emeritus,
University of Toronto

"The terrain that leaders of all stripes must now navigate has become increasingly complex, challenging and potentially depleting. The way through the darkest of hours is not only to find the light, but also to be the light. *The Empowering Leader* handily addresses this seemingly unaddressable truth with enough purity, clarity, and direction to make it useful to all who would consider such a prescription. Courage, taken from the French word *le coeur* meaning 'the heart,' is what is called for to address the grittiest of challenges, and acting on behalf of the greater good instead of self-interest or monetary gain requires a source of self-renewal and sustainability for both the leader and those who are following. This book provides a lifeline for continuing in the face of tremendous challenges to great leaders."

—**Alan M. Blankstein**, founder, Solution Tree and HOPE Foundation; author of *Failure Is Not an Option*

"Stephen and Paul are gifted storytellers and leaders. In this book, they open doorways to new ways of thinking that will stretch and widen any reader's capacity to inspire others. The world needs what they offer within these pages."

—**Dawna Markova**, PhD, author, *Collaborative Intelligence: Thinking with People Who Think Differently*

The Empowering Leader

12 Core Values to Supercharge Your Leadership Skills

Paul D. Houston
and
Stephen L. Sokolow

ROWMAN & LITTLEFIELD
Lanham • Boulder • New York • London

Published by Rowman & Littlefield
A wholly owned subsidiary of The Rowman & Littlefield Publishing Group, Inc.
4501 Forbes Boulevard, Suite 200, Lanham, Maryland 20706
www.rowman.com

Unit A, Whitacre Mews, 26-34 Stannary Street, London SE11 4AB

British Library Cataloguing in Publication Information Available

Library of Congress Cataloging-in-Publication Data Available

ISBN 978-1-4758-3354-6 (cloth : alk. paper)
ISBN 978-1-4758-3355-3 (pbk. : alk. paper)
ISBN 978-1-4758-3356-0 (electronic)

∞™ The paper used in this publication meets the minimum requirements of
American National Standard for Information Sciences—Permanence of Paper
for Printed Library Materials, ANSI/NISO Z39.48-1992.

Printed in the United States of America

This book is dedicated to

Steve's grandchildren:

Gabrielle & Sebastien
Lyla & Jonah

and

Paul's grandchildren:

Will & Lucy
Jade
Jackson & Annaleigh

Who represent our
best and brightest future

Contents

Foreword

While I served as governor of South Carolina and then later as United States Secretary of Education, I found that my own education as a leader was continuing. I learned many valuable lessons of what makes a leader effective, but I will mention just two here.

First, I learned that I was only as effective as those who worked around me. I always knew that leadership is getting work done through others, but when one leads a state government or a national department with thousands of employees, that lesson becomes crystal clear. The work of any leader is really the work of others. That requires the leader to constantly find ways of empowering others to see the work of the organization as their own and to find purpose in what they do.

Second, I learned that, as a government leader, anything I did would be magnified well beyond the walls of our organization. Therefore, I had to be driven by a deep sense of commitment to the values I learned while growing up because what I said and did had a real impact on others. Leaders play a symbolic role for those in their organizations and for those the organization serves. I needed to be clear in thought and deed because what I said and did would send ripples, large and small, out to others.

Productive leadership in any venue requires strength, passion, and commitment toward a vision. A good leader will possess core values and surround himself or herself with knowledgeable, fair-minded, and competent people. This improves the effectiveness of the leader, as well as nurturing and empowering the people within the organization.

We are living in a time when leaders are being challenged on all fronts. In this book, Paul Houston and Stephen Sokolow provide an outstanding set of core values to help guide leaders to meet those challenges successfully.

Richard W. Riley
Former U.S. Secretary of Education
Former Governor of South Carolina

Preface

The path to empowering leadership is a journey of discovery. It is a journey to discover who we are, what our gifts are, and how we can leverage our gifts to maximize our effectiveness. The purpose of the journey isn't just to improve ourselves, however. It is to improve those who work with us, too. This journey toward becoming the best version of ourselves allows us to find ways to bring out the best in others. By bringing out the best in our people and our organizations, we can actually supercharge them to go beyond what we might have dreamed they could become. This approach also allows our organizations to thrive in difficult times.

The authors of this book, Paul Houston and Stephen Sokolow, bring to the writing of this book more than forty years of leadership experience in successively more responsible roles at local and national levels. They are also the cofounders of the Center for Empowered Leadership. Over the years, both have observed and become increasingly aware that core values strengthen leadership. They have also observed that leaders who empower others seem to be more successful and have organizations that seem to thrive. By understanding the operating system of leadership that results from underlying core values, leaders equip themselves and those around them to turn stumbling blocks into stepping stones. They have the power to supercharge those around them.

If you have ever gone white-water rafting, you know what an exhilarating experience it can be. It is also a wonderful way to understand the feeling of leading in turbulent times. The role of the leader is to get his or her organization through the white water that surrounds them and to find the exhilaration of success that comes from getting past the rapids and into calmer waters. Paul learned many valuable leadership lessons on a white-water rafting trip. The first was how necessary collaboration is to success. Everyone on the raft has to do their part to keep the raft balanced and moving forward. Sometimes these roles are different, yet symbiotic. Often, the rapids are mastered by the folks on one side of the boat rowing forward while the ones on the other side row backward. This allows the raft to align with the natural flow of the river and, when done properly, to shoot through the rapids to calm water. Of course, if people aren't doing their jobs or are doing the wrong things at the wrong times, the raft spins and takes the rafters down the river backwards—affording a great view of where they have been but no sense of what lies ahead.

Another aspect of rafting is that it is often counterintuitive. You must act in ways that logically don't seem to make sense. Take the technique called "high siding," for instance, which is used when the raft hangs up on a rock. To free it, everyone on the raft moves to the side that is hung up. Logic would tell us that putting all the weight on one side would destabilize the raft and cause it to capsize, but the extra weight serves to offset the power of the river, allowing the raft to settle into the water and move forward.

Leading in today's world is very much like navigating, but merely surviving the journey isn't nearly good enough. Organizations must not merely survive—they need to thrive, and that is where empowering your organization comes into play. To create an atmosphere that supercharges your organization requires using all the skills and knowledge you have. But it requires even more than that. It requires you to be a certain kind of leader. To maintain your own balance and avoid capsizing your organization requires the ballast that comes from operating from a core set of values that allow constancy and consistency.

We can change the world. In fact, we *do* change our world each and every day. Usually these changes are small and subtle. Often, we are unaware of what we have done to create them. Lacking awareness sometimes means that the changes we create are the wrong changes. Leading with a sense of awareness allows us to make certain that our actions are thoughtful and positive. We share a basic value with you—we all want to make the world a better place.

Having and declaring this positive intention is a great place to start, but it is not enough. Declaring our intention to make the world a better place declares what we want to do. However, for this intention to grow in power, it must also include the why and how of making it so. Why do we want to do this, and how are we going to do it? The reasons that underlie our intention matter. Without action, we are left with mere wishful thinking.

By nature, we are optimists. We tend to see possibility and opportunity in the darkest of circumstances. We want to be clear about that because by almost any measure we would all have to admit there are many troubles in the world. We want to make the world better because everywhere you look, the urgent need for betterment is clearly evident. For us, making the world better carries both a practical and moral imperative. We are all affected by what is happening on our planet. In an interconnected world, each of us has an obligation—a moral imperative—to do all we can to make the world better. If we don't do our part, how do we expect others to do theirs?

So what's the key to shaping a better world? We offer two words—*empowering leadership*. It is not enough just to have better leadership or more effective leadership. We need empowering leadership that multiplies everyone's efforts. We believe that the whole is greater than the sum of its parts, and empowering our organizations creates a more powerful and better world because of the multiplier effect of common action.

In our last book, *The Wise Leader*, we took the position that wise leadership involves doing the right things in the right way, at the right time, for the right reasons. In this book we go further to suggest that it is not enough simply to be a wise leader—we must become empowering leaders. It has been said that the definition of leadership is getting work done through others. Empowering leadership supercharges this work—and the results of the work. A leader who cannot empower others is cheating the organization—and the world—of the full promise that collaboration can deliver.

We lay out a pathway for your journey to empowering leadership by offering twelve values that, when applied consistently, will make you a more empowering leader. These values should be familiar to you because you already possess them! They already exist, to varying degrees, in your conscious or your unconscious mind. By reading this book, you will be able to focus your attention more consciously and thoughtfully to grow these values within you. As you consciously choose to expand the practice of these core values in your style of leadership, you will become a more empowering leader. And as you empower those around you, you will find you are supercharging your organization with new energy and possibilities.

Each of the core values we present in this book is a seed. As we plant and nurture these seeds, we enable them to grow into the fruit and flowers of greater possibility. As the effects of empowering leadership ripple across our interconnected world, we will reap a better world for ourselves and our children.

May we empower our own and each other's paths to create a better and brighter future for our respective organizations and the world.

Acknowledgments

We are all the sum of what has touched us, and anything I might do is the result of what others have done for me. There are far too many to mention. I would like to thank my father, who grounded my spiritual beliefs with a sense of grace and generosity. He was the best Christian I have ever known because he got the "word" and made it "flesh." My mother gave me my warrior spirit and the common sense necessary to navigate this temporal plane. The late Richard Green made me see myself as more than my past, and my "Tucson Gang" (Rog, Vee, Jack, Sue, Ross, Suzy, Jesse, and Jackie) has been my family through thick and thin.

A number of spiritual guides have come to me when I needed them—the teachers who were there when the student was ready—and to each and all, I am most grateful. My children—Lisa, Suzanne, and Caroline—taught me that while we are connected to the Divine, that connection is played out in the chain of life that we receive and pass on to others; also, they make me laugh. I thank the universe for Sandra, who proved that it all comes in the right time and space and who has encouraged this work, and me, to become all that God intended. I want to express my gratitude to my grandchildren Will, Lucy, Jade, Jackson, and Annaleigh, who constantly remind me that we should all remember to approach life as a child—to be open to mystery and magic, to be optimistic beyond all reason, and to remain playful in the extreme. And finally, for Steve, whose focus and determination have kept this work alive and who has taught me more about spirituality and leadership than he might ever imagine.

Steve and I would both like to thank Jan Chapman, who early in this process took our hundreds of hours of mutual mumbling and made sense of it so that a manuscript could eventually emerge.

Paul D. Houston

Bringing this work to publication has been a synchronistic journey. It is a journey that Paul Houston and I began more than twenty-five years ago when we started swapping books with spiritual and mystical themes at Harvard University's summer seminar for superintendents. In an unplanned, inspired moment during the summer of 2000, Paul asked me if I would like to co-author a book with him about the integration of spirituality and leadership. During the next few years we collaborated on the spiritual principles of leadership in extensive weekly dialogues. Those dialogues became the foundation for our first two books, *The Spiritual Dimension of Leadership* and *The Wise Leader*, as well as this book.

I wish to express my heartfelt thanks to Paul for proffering an invitation that changed the course of my life. Our synergistic relationship demonstrates that the whole can indeed be greater than the sum of its parts. We have become close friends and partners in a venture that reaches beyond the horizon.

My well of gratitude runs deep with all of the people who have contributed to my life's path.

More than forty years ago, Professor Lee Olson first introduced me to the core values of leadership. He was a role model for what it means to truly live your values. I am indebted to him for his love and guidance and for being a stellar example of an empowering leader.

My brother Adam is a mystic and an advanced student of esoteric spiritual teachings from the East. For many years we have been taking "walk 'n' talks" in nature. He has been my guide, teacher, and executive coach. His wise counsel has been invaluable to my growth as a human being, and his insights have helped to shape my own.

I am a Reiki Master and have been practicing Reiki for more than twenty years. Reiki is a form of energy that promotes healing and spiritual growth. I am indebted to Djuna Wojton, a wonderful human being and Reiki Master who has shared her gift with me and countless others.

Alan S. Fellheimer is my lifelong friend. More than forty years ago when I was writing my first book—my doctoral dissertation—Alan taught me the craft of writing. Without his countless hours of tutorials, neither that book nor this one would have seen the light of day.

Fred Young and I shared distinguished honors in our doctoral program more than forty years ago. Fred is a gifted educator, scholar, and steadfast friend. As a former English teacher, he graciously edited this book.

Dr. Muska Mosston is a deceased friend whose spirit I still carry in my heart. A distinguished educator and author, he was like a second brother to me during the fifteen years when our lives converged. He loved the world of ideas, and he loved to write. As we talked about education and leadership, he continually urged me to write a book. He was the third in my rule of threes to suggest that I attend Harvard's summer seminar for superintendents. Without Muska, the synchronistic chain of events that lead to the writing of this book would have been broken.

My special thanks go to my wife, Laney, for her steadfast love, devotion, and encouragement to pursue my life's work, and also for her skills as a copy editor. Last, I want to thank our sons, Brett and Brian, who have been a continuing source of growth for me and who are the source of many insights incorporated into this work.

With heartfelt gratitude,
Stephen L. Sokolow

Introduction

The Empowering Leader is organized into twelve chapters, one chapter for each of the twelve core values designed to supercharge your leadership skills, and two bonus chapters! Bonus chapter 1 is The Gift of Synchronicity—Our Hidden Guidance System. The second bonus chapter is The Gift of Syntropy—Constructive Action. We call these two *gifts* because understanding them has been a gift to us, and we are honored to share those gifts with you. Each chapter opens with a brief overview of one of the twelve core values of empowering leadership. Short stories are interspersed throughout each chapter to illustrate the core values of empowering leadership in action. The content of each chapter is divided into from six to eleven subheadings. Each chapter concludes with a brief, bulleted inset summarizing the key concepts.

The chapters can be read in any order; each can stand alone. Similarly, each subheading within the chapter can stand alone. Some of our readers have opted to read a chapter each week in order to have sufficient time for reflection. The same approach can be taken with each subheading. We recommend reading this book in a manner, pace, and rhythm that works best for you.

The core values of empowering leadership described in this book are universal. Therefore, anyone in or aspiring to a leadership role would find this work enlightening and useful, including leaders in both the public and private sectors.

Many of the values, beliefs, and principles that guide and sustain leaders have underlying roots, which we call seeds of empowerment. The more closely we adhere to these seeds, the more empowering our leadership becomes, and the more effective we become in leading others to do their best.

The seeds of empowering leadership, which are the heart of this book, are available to all of us as leaders, and we increase our effectiveness if we embody them. These archetypal seeds are real, and they are accessible to each and every one of us.

Under the right conditions, seeds are planted and given the proper nutrients, which allows them to grow and fulfill their potential. This book contains countless seeds of empowering leadership that can resonate with the archetypal seeds that spring from within you. As you focus your attention on them, they will grow and flourish. As you set your intention to infuse them into your practice of leadership, they will grow. The more you think about them and talk about them, the stronger they will become. The more you use them, the stronger they will become. The more of them you incorporate into your practice of leadership, the more empowering you will become.

Just as a handful of acorns can grow into a cluster of oak trees, which in turn bear more acorns and, over time, become a forest, so too can the seeds of empowerment grow in you and propagate throughout your organization. As you practice—and ultimately come to embody—more and more seeds of empowerment, you will find yourself increasingly supercharged in your leadership skills, and you and your organization will be the better for it.

Identifying, Nurturing, and Using Our Unique Gifts and Talents

First, it was fingerprints, then voiceprints and retinal scans, and now DNA that shows that each human being is truly unique—a one-of-a-kind original. Yet that uniqueness is not just physical. Minds are unique and so are spirits. But uniqueness extends even further—each person has unique gifts and talents.

Part of our journey in life is to figure out what those gifts and talents are, how to cultivate them, and how to share them. But we can't do this selfishly because the final and most important step is to share them with others. Not only must leaders model this, but also they must facilitate this process in others. When you do this, you are empowering all those whose lives you touch.

EMPOWERING LEADERS ARE AWARE THAT EVERYONE HAS UNIQUE GIFTS AND TALENTS

We know of a school leader who early in his or her career was given line authority over the district's principals and supervisors. Emma, the supervisor for elementary education, had served in that role a long time and seemed to be coasting toward retirement.

Since this school leader was Emma's new boss, she approached him seeking "marching orders" for the year. She wanted to know what he wanted her to do. He told her to get out of the central office, go visit schools, and figure out how she might do the most good. She told him to quit kidding and to just tell her what to do. Her whole career had been one in which she waited for orders from her supervisor. Here she was being told to be *self-directed*. The leader wasn't just giving her permission to do this, he was insisting on it.

It was clear from what he heard from her and others that she had once been a master teacher and a gifted teacher of teachers. He told her he wanted her to use her natural gifts, that he trusted her, and that she should let him know if she ran into any difficulties.

That's when the magic happened. She began meeting with teachers and coaching them. She gave demonstration lessons and co-taught classes that burst into life. She chose to work with some of the most difficult students in the school. She became a cross between Johnny Appleseed and Florence Nightingale. She helped those in need and sowed seeds of loving kindness and joy wherever she went.

As the year ended, Emma asked the administrator if she could postpone her retirement; rediscovering her gifts and talents and sharing them with others had energized her. Several years later, she did retire, but she took a position training new teachers at a nearby college. She had been given the circumstances to cultivate and share her gifts. She was empowered.

Everyone has gifts and talents. We are just not always open to seeing them. People tend to seek out others who are often like themselves. This narrows our perspective, and we often miss what others bring to the table. All organizations do better when they celebrate and embrace their diversity. This is true on a number of levels. Diverse skills, attitudes, and worldviews broaden and deepen the thinking and actions of everyone.

Often, parents have no problem realizing and celebrating the differences between their children, but everyone is a child of the human family, and we each bring our own gifts to the table. Sometimes we miss this by seeing the "otherness" of others. We see people who we do not know or are not familiar with and think of them as strange or different. Sometimes it is difficult to appreciate that the "strangeness" of another is really a gift worth discovering and celebrating.

We even see this pattern happening in families. Sometimes one child does everything the parent wants, while another always seems to be at cross purposes with what is expected. But sometimes it is the "challenging" child that does something unusual and spectacular. They are just following a different path. Their unique perspective offers other gifts.

As a leader, you will be confronted by people who are more than a little different. Your challenge is to open yourself to their unique gifts and talents. People aren't different to be difficult; they are different because that is who they are.

EMPOWERING LEADERS DEVELOP
THEIR OWN GIFTS AND TALENTS

Education should always be about exploring what is out there, but as people get older, they forget they should keep exploring. They've fallen into a rut and live in it. In kindergarten, every child is an artist, a singer, a musician. As they get older, they lose that ability to see themselves as talented and they start to fear the journey. Leaders should never give in to their own fear of trying and failing.

Good advice for any young leader is to never polish the same side twice. If you are already good at something, stop polishing it. Go polish another side; that way you will be shiny all over. It is a constant struggle to fight against your natural instincts to stay with what you know and can do, because that is your comfort zone. Most people are much more talented than they will ever know.

One of the authors' mother told him early on that he was a natural teacher. She would say, "I look out the window and I see little children following you wherever you go and clinging to you. You seem to enjoy this. What I see is a natural teacher."

Later, he worked during the summer as a counselor at a camp for children with physical disabilities. One of the campers had a physical disability in his legs and short stumps for arms, but this camper wanted to learn to swim. The counselor set out to make this child's dream possible. He tried to put himself in the camper's place by trying to swim without using his own arms and legs. He discovered that he could swim by undulating his body like a dolphin. He figured out how to turn over in the water without using his arms or legs. He taught these skills to the boy. He put a life jacket on the boy, and the boy could flip himself into the pool, right himself, and swim across to the other side. The camper realized his dream of learning to swim.

This story teaches several lessons for the empowering leader. You have to be open to seeing others for who they are and what they're capable of doing. You have to accept their differences, and you have to be able to put yourself in their place. To empower others to find and develop their own gifts, you must see them as themselves and empathize with their challenges. Cultivating someone else's gifts is not imposing your own on them.

You need to seek out people who can be teachers to you and use them as mentors and role models. There is a teaching in Zen that when the student is ready, the teacher will appear. It is also true that when the teacher is ready, the student appears. Empowering leaders must be ready to empower.

EMPOWERING LEADERS HELP OTHERS CULTIVATE THEIR GIFTS AND TALENTS

One of the authors had a terrible time in school. In fact, he barely survived ninth grade. In his early years, he was considered a slow learner, and then in junior high, he rose to underachiever status. He made Ds and D-minuses in English, which was the cutoff for getting into high school.

The problem was that he was a holistic learner in a linear environment. It sometimes took a while for the pieces to fall into place. In high school that happened, and he started making straight As. He was classified as gifted. He was the same person he had always been, but the perception of him changed.

In tenth grade, he had a teacher named Mrs. Crum. One day after class, she asked him if he had ever thought about being a writer. He looked at her as if she had lost her mind. After all, he was the guy who had recently nearly failed ninth-grade English. Nevertheless, that conversation planted a seed. It became a pivotal moment for him and now several hundred articles and a handful of books later, he considers himself a writer. It was that moment of confirmation from Mrs. Crum that helped him recognize one of his gifts.

In life, it is often those little moments of affirmation that make the biggest difference. Part of recognizing unique gifts and talents is to see what is in front of you. Yogi Berra once said that you can observe a lot just by watching. You can also miss a lot by being self-centered. It is good to note that the opposite of the affirmation of talent is also powerful. Criticism and denigration can create a downward spiral and stifle talent.

Leaders need to be constantly aware that these little moments have huge consequences. In a single moment, you can make all the difference for another person. The difference you make can have profound influence and infinite reverberations. Most of us are where we are today because we were touched or affirmed by someone else.

Everyone has opportunities to help other people discover their unique gifts and talents, but this is especially true of leaders. Your impact may begin with a question, like the teacher who asked the student if he had considered being a writer, or it might be a positive comment that takes root. Your feedback gives people insight into their gifts and talents. Whether they have been told before, your comment, as a leader, can help them see themselves in new ways and can be a powerful impetus for action.

The cellist Pablo Casals once observed that rather than teaching children just facts and skills, we should teach children who they are. They should be reminded that they are "a marvel" and that they are unique and capable of anything. Wouldn't leaders be well served to plant those same seeds in those with whom they work?

Being gifted isn't about knowing mathematical formulas or the capitals of the world's nations. Rather, giftedness involves your humanity—what you have to offer at the human level. When leaders learn to identify and cultivate gifts in others, their organization becomes an empowering one. Empowering leaders have their radar set to spot the unique gifts and talents in their organization. Once they appear on the radar, those gifts need to be acknowledged and affirmed by being placed in the spotlight. Then the leader must find ways to allow these gifts to develop.

Sometimes this means putting people in a difficult situation. One leader we know took over the superintendency of a large school system and learned that one of the assistants was taking a leave of absence to pursue her doctorate. The assistant expected to return to her old position when the leave ended, but in the meantime, the leader had reorganized the district.

He told the assistant superintendent that her job supervising a number of schools was no longer there and instead she would be assigned to business and finance. She complained that she didn't know anything about business and finance. The superintendent told her he knew that but he also knew that she wanted to be a superintendent of an urban school district and that she would need to know those areas. This was particularly true because she was a minority and lingering racism often kept minorities away from controlling the money in school districts.

He also pointed out that she has already done the other job and needed to learn new skills. She had already polished that side. She was so angry that she only spoke to the superintendent in meetings. This went on for several months until one day she asked if she could meet with him. She told him that she wanted to thank him. She had found the last few months difficult and frustrating, but as she learned the skills needed in the new role, she realized it was also exhilarating.

She told the superintendent that making her take on that challenge was one of the best things that ever happened to her and that she had learned more in the last few months than she had in the last few years. She went on a few years later to become a very successful urban superintendent.

There are hidden assets that sometimes need to be uncovered. This assistant had skills she didn't know she had. There are also assets of potentiality where the ingredients exist but have to be put together. Leaders can create circumstances in which people can develop these assets further.

In another school district in the mid 1980s, there was a chemistry teacher who wrote a mini grant proposal to purchase a computer so he could conduct chemistry experiments simulating certain chemical reactions for his students. The superintendent suggested he craft his proposal to create a twenty-five-station lab that would benefit the whole department. The teacher won the grant and created the first computer lab in the district. He learned so much about computers doing this that he eventually became the district's technology director. He went on to learn about the Internet and created the first wide area networks in the whole region, linking thousands of computers. His life and the district's success were changed because the leader had helped him see a greater potential.

EMPOWERING LEADERS FACILITATE
THE SHARING OF GIFTS AND TALENTS

Leaders are like ringmasters in the circus. They present the show and separate out the different acts or events so they are coherent for the audience. They direct attention to different acts. They point out that the lions are in ring two and that the jugglers are in ring three. They make sure that the jugglers aren't in the lion's cage! Leadership is sorting out the pieces and putting the spotlight in the right place.

Another element of leadership is to facilitate the sharing process so that everyone's talents can be understood and appreciated. Leadership is in the sense-making business. The leader must find a way to get all the gifts and talents in the organization sorted out and spotlighted.

Part of this process is to find the right showcase for the talents of the staff. They need to help the organization know and appreciate the multidimensional qualities that are everywhere in the organization. Maybe the CEO's assistant has a beautiful singing voice. While it is not in her job description to sing, perhaps the leader can find a way to show the others in the organization her special talent. This reinforces her value to the organization and helps others see her in a new way.

People have gifts that extend beyond those needed for their responsibilities and positions. Empowering leaders learn how to discover and cultivate these gifts, at least to the point of showcasing them so others can appreciate the wide range of gifts that others have. Sometimes people make judgments on what is appropriate. Someone might think it isn't appropriate for the assistant to sing. This judgment builds walls in the organization and creates a hierarchical way of thinking. It is the leader's task to tear down these boundaries.

We know of one school leader who asked the staff in his organization to tell him if they had a gift or talent they wanted to share with their students. He included bus drivers, custodians and secretaries. The results were amazing. He found out the director of maintenance was an expert fly-fisherman who wanted to teach students fly-fishing. A guidance counselor worked on weekends as a sportscaster for professional basketball and he introduced the students to that world.

These were the results of asking a simple question and giving people permission to reveal who they were and what they had to offer. If you make it OK for people to bring more of who they are into the workplace, it enriches not only them but also the organization.

EMPOWERING LEADERS EXTEND GIFTS AND TALENTS

Sometimes it all comes down to sharing the wealth. When you fail to share, you limit your effectiveness. We know a leader who went on a trip to Africa. He noticed that the warthogs, the wildebeests, and the zebras all seemed to stay together. He asked the naturalist about this. He wondered if they just liked each other or what was happening. The naturalist explained that one had better eyesight, one had better hearing, and one had a better sense of smell. Each had weaknesses offset by one of the other's strengths. By being together, they combined their natural strengths and protected each other. This is a wonderful lesson in collaboration and strength from diversity.

We all have strengths and weaknesses. These weaknesses are often the darker side of our gifts and talents. By working together and by embracing those around you in partnership and collaboration, you are able to share your strengths and benefit from theirs. This can also cover up some of your weaknesses. Like the warthog, the wildebeest, and the zebra, you have each other's backs.

When you look for partners, you should look beyond those who are compatible with you to those who might complement you. The better you know your own strengths and weaknesses, the easier it will be to find powerful partnerships with those who complement you.

One of the authors and his brother have very different strengths and weaknesses, but they have found this builds a stronger bond between them and makes them more effective. The synergy they create yields better results than if they worked alone. There is a reason the idea of "opposites attract" has become a cliché. It carries some wisdom.

This understanding of complementarities is particularly important in building teams in the workplace. Empowering leaders select people whose strengths complement each other. This brings out the best in each individual and builds a stronger team. By working together, they create a whole greater than the sum of its parts.

UNIQUENESS CONTRIBUTES TO THE TAPESTRY OF LIFE

People have different colors and textures, and the variation among them when blended harmoniously can create a tapestry. When harmony is not present, it leaves a pile of rags. If you hang a sheet on the wall, it isn't interesting. It is the same color, same size threads, and even dimensions. On the other hand, a tapestry with variation in color and kinds of thread can be a work of art.

Most of us are familiar with George Washington Carver's scientific achievements, but we may not know that Carver was also an artist. Carver loved to walk along the back roads of rural Alabama near his Tuskegee home and on his walks he would find castoff items along the road.

He would collect the twine, yarn, and bits of string he found and would take them home. He would find interesting colors of clay. He would scoop it up and collect it for later. When he had enough twine, yarn, and string he would weave tapestries, and when he had enough clay, he would use it to make watercolor paint and would paint lovely pictures with it. These tapestries and paintings now hang in museums.

This creative recycling demonstrated that even the lowliest castoff material can become precious. Finding unique talents is discovering the precious in those around you, even when it might appear there is little value there. Sometimes by blending together disparate items, you can create a unique work of art. The richness of the differences helps create the value.

Imagine what a landscape would look like if every flower and tree were exactly the same. Differences create the beauty and power of nature. Differences also create beauty and power in humans. Our uniqueness contributes to the tapestry of life by contributing to the larger whole. In each of our roles, we express different aspects of ourselves, and these differences create the larger picture.

To use a different metaphor, each of us is a piece in a greater puzzle. The puzzle isn't complete until each piece finds its place. Each person is unique and until each person's gifts are discovered and cultivated one cannot complete the whole. Empowering leaders make certain that all the pieces are used and that all the pieces are placed properly. This empowers each piece.

OUR HIGHER POWER HELPS CLARIFY LIFE'S PURPOSE(S)

It may seem strange to see our *higher power* referenced in a book on leadership, but we believe that there is an infinite cord that connects all of us to each other and to the deeper parts of ourselves. This connection is expressed in different ways in different traditions, but for our purposes here we will refer to it as our *higher power*.

Sometimes people spend their time invalidating and ignoring the gifts they have been given. Yet, we keep getting signals that we should go forth and develop ourselves. This is easy to see in others, but much tougher to see in ourselves. We need to pay attention to the signals we get.

There are signals everywhere for us, telling us what we should do and how we should do it, but we ignore them out of convenience or ignorance. For example, there is a story about a man who is trapped in a flood, and he calls out to God for help. Minutes later, a log goes floating by, but the man lets it go. The waters continue to rise and a boat comes along. The person in the boat offers to help the man by picking him up, but the man declines telling the man that he is waiting for God to save him. The water continues to rise. A helicopter flies over and the pilot calls out to the man. Again, he declines the help explaining he is waiting for God to save him. Finally, the waters rise over the man's head and he drowns. Upon getting to heaven, he demands that God explain why he hadn't saved him. He was a man of faith, and God let him die. God points out that he sent a log, a boat, and a helicopter and wondered why the man didn't see the help when it was right in front of him.

Like the man in the flood, people tend to look for help from a *higher power* without understanding that most of the time there will not be miraculous intervention but that help is there nonetheless. To an extent, help is our higher power and our gifts and ability to access others' gifts through cooperation. You need to use your senses, your feelings, the thoughts that come to you through your intuition and the information you gather and then ask yourself if there is a message there for you. Then it is time to act.

Saint Francis of Assisi once said, "If you work with your hands, you are a laborer. If you work with your hands and head, you are a craftsman. But if you work with your hands, your head, and your heart and your soul, you are an artist." So the challenge for the empowering leader is to find a way to access the heart and soul in her work. Those are ultimately the talents you should pursue for yourself and for those you lead and serve.

TO BECOME A MORE EMPOWERING LEADER

- Be aware that everyone has unique gifts and talents.
- Discover and develop these unique gifts and talents.
- Help others cultivate their unique gifts and talents.
- Facilitate the sharing of these gifts and talents.
- Extend your own unique gifts and talents.
- Understand how uniqueness contributes to the tapestry of life.

Core Value 2

Understanding and Manifesting Our Intention

Leaders confront endless challenges and opportunities as they chart the future for their organizations. One of the most powerful tools you have at your disposal is your own intention. Knowing that your intention is a powerful force allows you to focus in ways that will help you translate your ideas into reality and bring about the positive changes you envision.

INTENTION IS A FUNDAMENTAL
CORE VALUE OF EMPOWERING LEADERSHIP

Almost everything we do starts with an intention. Intention is a framework for the creation of reality. It's the building plans for reality. Before you can have a plan, you've got to have an intention: the thought of what you want to see happen or where you want to go or what your ultimate goal is. From that beginning, you can start developing plans.

Sending the intention out to the universe creates energy. It creates an energy cycle that is largely outside of your control once you send it out. So you're not just acting from your own center of power; you're also enlisting the aid of a lot of other seen and unseen powers outside of you, stirring up the pot of energy that the universe makes available when you create a sense of what you want to do and why you want to do it.

You can think of an intention as the ripples of a stone skipping along the surface of a pond. Each time it touches the pond, the stone generates a series of ever-expanding concentric circles, and the sets of circles intersect and overlap at some point. The pattern created by intention is similar to the surface of the pond after the stone passes through, but because the medium is life and not water, the reverberations travel like light and do not lose strength as they contribute to the fabric of life.

Most leaders do not have a strong enough appreciation of the power of intention as a force for shaping reality. People do or want to do so many things that it's not always clear what their intentions are. It's very important for leaders to have clear in their own mind what their intentions are—not only what they would like to see happen in a particular set of circumstances or in a particular dynamic but also what motivation lies one step beneath the goal itself.

Besides knowing what your goals are in any given set of circumstances, you should, to the extent that it is possible, ask yourself about your primary motivation. This is a personal process between you and your inner or higher self. That internal dialogue about what you want to do and why you want to do it ignites the spark that goes out into the universe as an energy field.

For example, you could have a goal to lose weight, but the intention is to be healthy. The intention is more fundamental than the goal. The intention can even create a set of goals. The goals themselves are not the intention; the intention is underneath the goal and explains why. Why would *you* want to be healthy beyond the fact that everyone does? Your intention to be healthy may tie into your need to have sufficient energy to make a more positive contribution to the world or to meet your professional responsibilities. So intention ties into a more fundamental set of reasons about why you want to do something.

As leaders, the intentions that carry the most force are the ones that will benefit people other than ourselves. But that doesn't mean that your intentions can't also benefit you. You can benefit from being healthy, but by being healthy, you are in a better position to serve others.

THOUGHT IS MORE IMPORTANT THAN PEOPLE THINK

Why is thought more important than you think? Thought is the "Energizer Bunny" for what happens. Like most people, you may assume that what you think is private; it doesn't go anywhere and just rattles inside your head. You figure you can have these thoughts and not have any impact. But the reality is that a thought creates a force of energy that immediately goes beyond your head and out into the world at large. When you create a thought, that thought immediately leaves your being and goes out into the universe where it has the potential to start manifesting itself in activities and results.

Believing that thoughts are private, most people assume that they're free to think outlandish things and maybe even hurtful things, and that thought is a harmless way of mentally processing options and choices. Yet, over our years of work together, we've come to understand that your thoughts function in a number of powerful ways. One is that your thoughts send messages not only to your body but also to your spirit, affecting both. Another is that thought itself sets up energy patterns that you transmit. While we don't understand precisely how this occurs, we are convinced that thoughts can even be picked up by others under certain circumstances and by spiritual forces as well.

It's been reported that more than 80 percent of the people in America believe in the power of prayer, and prayer—whether it is spoken, written, or silent—involves thought. Unless you think that only certain types of thought project out into the universe and the other ones are contained, you're left with the idea that all your thoughts radiate out. Where do they go? Do they just emanate out like a radio signal that gets fainter and fainter the further it travels? Or are they received and even recorded?

There is a mystical school of thought that holds the belief that all thoughts, words, and deeds are recorded in another plane of existence known as the astral realm in something called the Akashic Record. In this view, thoughts not only radiate out but are also stored. We know of no evidence that supports the existence of the Akashic Record, but the concept of being held accountable, at death, for how you lived your life exists in many religious traditions.

If there's no record, what's the mechanism for doing that? The whole notion of being judged at the end of life at least raises the question as to whether people are going to be judged not only by their deeds but by their thoughts as well. Such notions might serve as a motivation to direct thoughts in more positive ways and, because thoughts affect the people who think them, to replace negative thinking (what we colloquially call *stinkin thinkin*) with fruitful thinking.

Another reason that thought is more important than you think is that if you have one kind of thought pattern and try to act in another way, you create incredible cognitive dissonance. That disruptive pattern between thought and action is easily picked up by those around you. If you're trying to be one way and you're thinking another way, it's no secret to anybody around you. At a bare minimum, others know that something is in conflict; that what you're trying to create in terms of your outward behavior is at odds with who you are internally.

SPOKEN AND WRITTEN WORDS ARE KEYS TO MANIFESTING INTENTIONS

The spoken word is like an accelerant. It takes thought and accelerates it. It's like pouring kerosene on a fire. You could have a fire without the kerosene, but if you pour the kerosene on, it's going to build faster. The spoken word creates a power on top of the power that's already there, in essence, by taking your thought from one level to the next level. By speaking aloud, you've upped the ante. You can take it a further step by writing your intention or creating a visual representation of it. There are different ways of bringing energy to an intention, and you can keep escalating the energy by being more and more concrete and more physical.

Thoughts have power. Expressing those thoughts verbally steps up the power. Everyone has intentions, especially leaders who want to change the status quo. So one way of beginning the process of manifesting your intentions is to state them aloud.

When you do that, the question becomes "Who's listening and who's the audience?" When you speak aloud, is it in a closed room or a room full of people? Should you share your intention via radio and television? Should you say it aloud to the universe metaphysically? You need to have in mind not only what you would like to manifest but also who you want to hear your words to create the opportunity for other people and forces to assist you in manifesting your intentions.

The process of saying things aloud also helps to clarify your thinking and state your intention clearly. When you speak it aloud, you're raising a posse. You're enlisting support and the aid of others, whether you mean to or not, simply by sharing it. You've brought those who hear you into the circle of intention at that point; you've invited them into your place. In doing so, you've created the possibility of their helping you.

In terms of an energy level, a thought process has a pretty high frequency. When you express a thought in spoken words, you've lowered the frequency and created more reverberation. When you go to the level of the written word, you've lowered the frequency even further because you put your thought into a physical form that can be felt and touched.

Everything in the universe is made up of energy, but the energy operates at different frequencies. The spoken word is a different frequency than the thought word, and the written word is a different frequency than the spoken word. Each one vibrates at a lower and lower level. As you turn your thought to spoken and written words, you are creating more potential to bring your intention into reality simply by creating a vibrational field.

That's why leaders benefit not only by stating their intentions but also by writing them down. After writing them down, you need to share what you have written in as many forums as possible. The very act of writing your intention down helps to clarify your thinking. When people react to what you have written, their reactions can help you refine what you are writing so that it better conveys your meaning. At times, when people read what you write, they interpret it in ways you never intended. Having your intention in writing allows you to refine and clarify it so that it becomes crystal clear. Having it in written form makes it easier to share and increases the likelihood that your message will be conveyed as intended.

EMPOWERING LEADERS MUST ALIGN
THEIR ACTIONS AND INTENTIONS

Integrity is about "walking your talk," which relates to the alignment between what you do and what you say. Empowering leaders must also have an alignment between their intentions and what they do.

If you have an intention that you're serious about but then behave counter to it, you are certainly undercutting the likelihood of bringing it into reality. At times, people find their intentions inconsistent with their actions. We have found that when our intentions and actions are in alignment, our intentions tend to manifest themselves more quickly.

You, too, can end up seeing some results very quickly once you apply your actions to your intention, and so it's again taking it to that next level by saying, "All right, I've got this intention. Now I'm going to act on this intention to make it happen." A lot of effective motivational programs operate from the principle of creating your intentions and then acting on them—and keep acting on them in a consistent manner to make them happen. The fact is if you follow that technique, it's very powerful.

The acting consists of speaking, writing, and doing. Once you have your intentions clear and your potential actions employing those three elements aligned with your intention, then you have increased the power in a way that really increases the likelihood you will manifest your intention. There's certainly no guarantee, but when speaking, writing, and doing are aligned with your intention, you increase the probability of transforming your intention into something real.

This happens in part because other people are in a position to observe what you say, write, and do in relation to your professed intentions. The more consistent you are and the more resolve you show, the more others can determine the extent to which they identify with and support your stated intentions. When your intentions are honorable and focused on the common good, you tend to increase your ability to attract allies and resources that can assist you in the process of moving forward.

ENLISTING SPIRITUAL AND NONSPIRITUAL
FORCES TO MANIFEST INTENTIONS

Leaders would all like to manifest their intentions. Given the obstacles they must overcome, heaven knows leaders can use all the help they can get. By speaking about your intentions and sharing them with the world at large, you can consciously and unconsciously enlist spiritual and nonspiritual forces as allies. You can also enlist spiritual forces directly through prayer or meditation or whatever you might do to put yourself in touch with higher powers. For the nonspiritual forces—in other words, other people—the key is to create an understanding on their part of where you're trying to go.

There's something magnetic about powerful intention. People are drawn to it. People who really know where they're trying to go will draw folks to them, whereas people who are confused about where they're trying to go are not terribly magnetic. There is something to be said for the people who have clarity in their sense of where they want to go because they're able to draw support and people toward what they're trying to make happen. When you talk about empowering leadership, that's really what it's all about. It's drawing folks toward a vision or a dream. Essentially, intention is about creating dreams and possibilities that you want to see manifest in physical reality.

If your intention is clear, that in and of itself becomes an attractor. It's as though the intention sets up an energy field that serves as an attractor to other forces and energies. With respect to spiritual forces, you must first decide if you believe in them. If you don't, you can just focus on the nonspiritual forces. But if you are open to the notion that there are spiritual forces, consider that there are two types: internal and external.

People call internal spiritual forces their soul, their higher self, their spirit, or their divine spark; if you believe in them, then you would certainly be interested in enlisting them. Furthermore, if you believe that those internal forces are connected to forces outside of yourself, such as God, angels, archangels, deities, and so forth, you may choose to enlist those as well. Unless it's contrary to your beliefs, it's good to remain open to the possibility that there are spiritual forces in the universe that can be enlisted to help manifest your intentions. In our own lives, we not only have felt comfortable enlisting spiritual forces personally but also have found it very beneficial to do so.

People believe in a wide range of spiritual entities, including those that can be harmful as well as those that can be helpful. This is why it is so important to be clear about your intention. There's power in clarity—there's so little of it in the world at large. A lot of the world is pretty murky. When you have a sense of clarity about things, can communicate it to other people, and you can create that communication within yourself in terms of where you want to go and why, it acts as an attractor for people because they see the clarity in what you say.

We have been far more powerful in the times when we've had a sense of clarity about what we wished to see happen as opposed to having a sense of confusion or uncertainty about it. When you're unclear, you're all over the place; when you're clear, the path becomes clearer, too. As the mystical golfing caddy Bagger Vance put it, "It's seeing the field." It's knowing your destination and the path to it. When you have that, not only do you have the power, but circumstances align themselves around you to enhance that power as well.

USING THE "THIRD EYE" TO MANIFEST INTENTIONS

Your "third eye" is sometimes called the "mind's eye." It's what you have in the back of your mind as you are living your life day by day. For example, if you have an intention to create a collaborative environment for your staff, then as you look at events that come your way, you apply an additional lens, a lens that comes from that third eye to see in any given situation how you can use that circumstance to move your intention forward. The third eye is a lens that functions like a sixth sense that's available to you when you're trying to manifest a particular intention.

Leaders are always looking at the landscape, looking at the things that are coming toward them; and the things that they create not only help them to see what's happening but also help to determine how the situation could be used in manifesting a particular intention. It's another way of saying, "How do you hold the vision of your intention in the background of your consciousness as you're carrying out your responsibilities as a leader?"

The third eye is related to the whole notion of foreground and background. Foreground only has meaning if there is a background. To some extent, the third eye creates that bigger frame. It fills in those background spaces to allow what you're conscious of to have more sharpness. It allows what you're seeing to stick out because it has something to stick out from. Your third eye is also your intuitive sense, a sort of knowing without knowing how you know. When you have that enlisted along with the more conscious knowing that goes with overt attention, that's a pretty powerful combination.

One of the things that's wonderful about the third eye is that it sees in two directions: both inwardly and outwardly. It can see inwardly in terms of intuition and insight that come from spiritual sources, but it is also there seeing events and circumstances in light of your goals and intentions. Whenever the foreground presents you with the opportunity to shape events and move them in the direction of what you see in the background of your mind, you're using your third eye to do that. This ongoing process helps to manifest your intentions.

It's the difference between a window and a mirror to some extent. A window allows you to see in both directions—you can look out or you can look in through a window. In a mirror, you can see only what is reflected back at you. You don't get the full flavor of what's possible. When people operate in the conscious world, they tend to operate often with mirrors because they have created blind spots that only allow them to see one way. But when you operate on a higher plane, one that's more open to this other part of you involving your third eye, then the light goes in both directions.

EMPOWERING LEADERS USE ATTENTION
TO FOCUS THE LENS OF INTENTION

Intention and attention are two related forces that are both powerful. These forces complement each other, and either one can start the process. If you form an intention, you can use your attention to help manifest it. On the other hand, your attention may allow you to see a pattern, which then triggers the formation of an intention to do something about the pattern you have observed. Once you have an intention, there are many approaches that can help you manifest it in physical reality.

Earlier we suggested using your thought processes, using writing, using the spoken word, enlisting people, enlisting other organizations, enlisting spiritual forces, and so forth. One of the ways of enlisting these other forces is through your attention. When you give an intention more of your time and more airtime by using your position to promote it, you're giving it more of your energy; you are highlighting it, shining a light on it and toward it.

Picture an image, from an earlier time, of the town crier, who would walk through the town shouting out the news as people gathered around and listened. The town crier had the intention of bringing the news, but it was the sound of his bellowing voice that got people to focus their attention on it.

You've got to pay attention to get the intention going. Attention allows you to gather up that which is important and use it in a way that manifests something. You've got to gather the seed and put the seed in the basket before you sow. Attention is gathering the seeds, putting them in the basket, and planting them whereas manifested intention is the sowing of the fruit. If you can't get some attention going, it's very difficult to get the intention flowing.

Your intention starts as an idea or a feeling, or, perhaps, some combination of the two. It is something you want to see happen or come about in a way that is tangible. The many ways you have of attracting energy and giving energy to your intention all can be considered forms of attention. And you can increase the likelihood of manifesting your intention by increasing the attention you yourself bring to it as well as the attention you engender in others.

EMPOWERING LEADERS FOCUS
ENERGY TO MANIFEST INTENTIONS

Everybody has intentions, but a lot of them are petty intentions. They just don't amount to very much because people don't invest in them. You've probably heard, "I intend to be rich." To which we say, "OK, but what do you intend to do about it? What's the plan here? Where are you going with this?"

You might hear in response, "Well, I'm just sort of intending. You know, I'm buying lottery tickets." A lot of people buy the lottery tickets of life hoping that will get them where they want to go, but unless you follow up on your intentions by acting on them, you're not going anywhere.

A wealthy person who believed most people don't really want to be wealthy once said, "Sure, everybody wants to be wealthy. If wishing could make it so," as in, "I wish to wake up wealthy tomorrow by winning the lottery or receiving an inheritance." But like this man, many wealthy people not only work long hours at an extremely intense pace, including most weekends, to acquire their wealth, but also take substantive risks, and this requires another level of commitment. "There's a price to be paid, and most people aren't willing to pay that price," the wealthy friend added. In other words, there must be a complete alignment between your intention and your actions over time.

Leaders have an arsenal of energy available to them to manifest their intention. They can allocate resources such as time, money, and people. They can use their relationships and connections inside and outside of their organizations as well as the things we've already mentioned, from creating working groups and establishing priorities to prayer.

Leaders who seriously want to manifest a particular intention need to keep focusing on it over a sustained period of time and use their creativity to move toward it with relentless determination at every opportunity. Wishful thinking won't do it, but leaders have the resources to focus their own energy and the energy of others as well as spiritual energy to help them manifest their intentions. This is especially true when they are focusing on intentions that serve others and the common good.

Powerful intention has to have commitment attached to it. You may have an intention for something, but you've got to be committed to that intention. That commitment leads to action. You may have an intention of being healthy and losing weight, but if you haven't committed to that by creating an exercise program, an eating program, and so forth, you're not going to see a lot of manifestation of your intention. As the wealthy person above said, "Unless you're committed to becoming wealthy, you're probably not going to see it happen." You've got to go beyond "Wouldn't it be nice?"

Getting the thought sets the forces of the universe in motion and creates the possibility of help. Remember the old notion that heaven helps those who help themselves? That means your personal commitment. If you're not committed to making your intention manifest, enlisting everybody else's help in the process, either physically or spiritually, is not going to get you there.

So the first step is to make the commitment to the intention yourself. By doing that and by stating and writing the intention, you're putting it out into the universe to happen. Now you've got a powerful force at work because you have your own energy committed to making it happen, and you have enlisted the help of everything else in the universe to bring it forth as well.

TO BECOME A MORE EMPOWERING LEADER

- See intention as a fundamental core value.
- Know that thought is more important than people think.
- Use spoken and written words to manifest your intentions.
- Align your actions and intentions.
- Enlist spiritual and nonspiritual forces to manifest your intentions.
- Use your "third eye" to manifest your intentions.
- Use attention to focus the lens of your intention.
- Focus energy to manifest your intentions.

Using Affirmation to Make Things Happen

Affirmations come in all shapes and sizes. They range from simple declarations that you will do something like take out the trash or lose weight to written affidavits and sworn testimony under oath. Your signature on a check or contract is an affirmation that you are bound by law to honor its terms. Legal and religious institutions make extensive use of affirmations in various forms. Beyond their legal power, affirmations have the power to affect other people and our own behavior. We believe that affirmations create an energy that empowering leaders can use to impact positively on themselves and others.

AFFIRMATION IS AN IMPORTANT
CORE VALUE FOR EMPOWERING LEADERS

An affirmation creates or reinforces an intention for what you want to accomplish. In essence, it strengthens and amplifies your thought. It is one thing to think about something you should do or want to do, but when you use an affirmation, you are putting more energy into it and boosting its strength.

Think about the word itself—*affirmation*—which is derived from the word *affirm*. *Affirm* contains the root word *firm*, which is the opposite of the word *soft*. It is strong. It is a word with strength to it. When you affirm something, you're adding strength to it. We've written about intentions and the way empowering leaders strive to make things better. When you affirm an intention, you essentially create a vow and add real strength to it, which makes it much more than just a good thought. When you send that out to the universe, it creates an energy field that, like a magnet, attracts the elements needed to assist you in turning your affirmation into reality.

An affirmation is a form of a vow. It's a vow we make at three levels: (1) we make it to ourselves, (2) we make it to other people, and ultimately, (3) we make it to the universe and our higher power. It starts as a form of self-talk, a vow or a promise to our self to commit to a particular course of action, behavior, or goal. The power of an affirmation is directly proportional to our commitment to it. If we are committed to what it is we are affirming, at some point, we may choose to share our affirmation with other people. That has a way of reinforcing it and a way of helping us hold ourselves accountable for our own affirmation. Ultimately, we are affirming to the universe a particular action, goal, or promise, and that opens a gateway for help from both spiritual and nonspiritual forces.

SPEAKING SILENTLY TO ONESELF CAN BE A USEFUL FORM OF AFFIRMATION

Often, when we are thinking, we subvocalize. We are thinking but not being completely silent; we're right on that edge between being silent and audible. A person nearby might even ask you whether or not you know that you are talking to yourself. This is a form of self-talk. We encourage you to make your self-talk positive.

You might say things like, "I can do this" or "I want to do this" or "I will do this." You are making commitments to yourself. We firmly subscribe to the notion of a mind, body, spirit connection. When you engage in self-talk, you are alerting your body, mind and spirit of your intention. By formulating your thoughts and self-talk in a positive way, you are projecting an internal vision of the reality you want to create. In their optimal form, affirmations state things as though they are already true.

For example, instead of saying to yourself, "I'm going to lose ten pounds," you say, "I'm ten pounds lighter." It becomes an advanced version of reality as though it is already achieved. You may choose to speak silently or very close to silently in an affirmative way about things that are important to you.

People generally don't use affirmations for routine aspects of living; rather they tend to use them for things that are of special importance. We also find that people who are trying to develop a new habit (or break a bad one) can use an affirmation in that way as well. Instead of subvocalizing, "I want to stop smoking," you might say, "I no longer smoke."

Empowering leaders are optimistic and resilient. Positive self-talk may be the wellspring of those attributes. Your sense of optimism and resilience may flow from what you say to yourself about those qualities. When you're confronted with disappointment or difficulties, you can start by talking to yourself about what you plan to do about those circumstances. See things as you want them to be and the role you can play to bring that about. The seeds of empowering behaviors often start with the self-talk that you engage in.

The inverse is also true. Self-talk of a negative nature can reinforce and increase the probability of negative outcomes. When you find yourself in a negative space, you can use positive self-talk to reframe the situation, to envision how you can turn the situation around and focus on where you want to go. Our unconscious mind tends to believe what we tell it. The more we tell it the truth we would like to see, as though it is already true, the more we, as empowering leaders, can help shape the reality we want to experience.

SPEAKING ALOUD CAN BE A
USEFUL FORM OF AFFIRMATION

Once a thought is spoken, it becomes more real. It's the second step down the road to making something happen. We think so quickly that giving voice to our thoughts forces us to increase our clarity. When speaking aloud, we take more care to be sure that what we are saying is what we intend to say, especially when others are listening. Some affirmations work very well at the self-level when spoken out loud, such as, *I am healthy and happy*.

We jokingly say that people who talk to themselves are a little crazy, but that depends on what you are saying. If you are saying things that are life enhancing for yourself and for other people, then it is certainly a good thing to do rather than a problem.

As we get more comfortable with sharing what it is we are committed to doing we can increase the circle of awareness with respect to other people. Every time we verbalize that there is a particular thing we are working on, whether it is changing some aspect of our self or a goal, behavior, or a belief, it affirms our own commitment to it and lets others know what we are committed to doing.

As we use the spoken word and other people hear it, they may repeat it to others. That's one way we begin to get a multiplier effect in terms of energy, because they're not just hearing it; they are also sharing it with other people. They might say, "I was in a room when the boss said we ought to be focusing on such and such as leaders." As they share that, the affirmation begins the process of growing exponentially.

When you say something aloud, you open yourself up to being held accountable for what you say. As a case in point, a seventh-grade student described one of his teachers as chastising him for eating in class. She said it was simply rude to eat when other people weren't eating. He took her at her word. At the end of the day during homeroom, he collected money from his classmates to purchase twenty-five hoagie sandwiches. He bought them in the next morning and asked the cafeteria staff to store them until noon and then bring them to his class.

A little before noon, he took out a sandwich and started eating. The teacher said, "I thought I told you that it was rude to eat unless everybody else was eating at the same time." At that point, a cafeteria worker brought in twenty-five sandwiches and one for the teacher. The teacher was flabbergasted, but she knew her word was being tested. Everyone wound up eating hoagies during her class that day. The teacher said, "I can see I have to watch what I say in this class," and jokingly added, "Gee, I wish I had a new car." The student was testing whether the teacher would live up to her word.

That's what the universe does to us all the time. Are we really serious about what we mean and do we mean what we say? People listen to what empowering leaders say. They actually go out and try to do the things the leader espouses.

When you affirm things, you better mean what you say.

USING WRITING AND OTHER
VISUAL ARTS IN AFFIRMATION

In ancient Egypt, at least as it is depicted in the movies, the pharaoh says, "So let it be written. So let it be done." Putting something in writing made it official; made it more concrete and easier to share. Putting your thoughts in writing forces you to become increasingly accurate about that which you intend, hope, or plan. When you affirm something in writing, you create greater clarity.

We are our own first audience. First, we must satisfy ourselves that our words are aligned with our thoughts and feelings. The next step is to share our affirmation with others. We can start with our immediate family and then branch out to friends and trusted colleagues. We can then expand our circle to others in increasingly larger venues.

What form should it take? We are only limited by our imagination and creativity in terms of the form we use. It may be in the form of a note, list, or poem. We can also use other visual arts. Many people relate well to symbols, graphics, collages, or other forms of imagery that represent a goal or a vision of something we want to create. These are tools that you, as an empowering leader, can use to help manifest your intentions.

We created a graphic in the form of a visual map of the things we wanted to accomplish at the Center for Empowered Leadership. Showing that graphic to other people and seeing it ourselves increasingly crystallizes what we had in mind from a general notion to something that becomes more and more real. Certainly, a picture has a greater feeling of reality than something you just describe with words. There are people who are very comfortable drawing things. They use images of what it is they would like to create.

We can also use artifacts. As we write these words, we are involved in a storytelling process. When we were in Sedona, Arizona, we found little clay storytellers created by the indigenous people. They serve as a reminder to us of the importance of telling stories to illustrate the core principles about which we are writing. People ascribe meaning to a wide array of visual arts, which may not convey the same thing to me as they do to you, but as you explain what it means to you, you have another vehicle for reinforcing what it is that you are affirming.

The written word, spoken word, and images all create the possibility for synchronicity (see bonus chapter 1) and synergy. When you share your ideas of what you want to make happen, you discover other people who are interested, and have thoughts about what they might contribute, or connections that they have that can lead us toward our vision.

Again, affirmation is not just about creating the intention of doing something, but it's actually starting the building process. It's starting to put the structure in place simply by putting it out there. Some people sit around and dream. They don't put clothes on their dreams. You've got to put clothes on your dreams, take them out for a walk, and show them off to the world so that people can relate to them and help make them real.

You can think of it as a form of modeling. We formulate mental models and then paint pictures with our words and make visual models of what it is we want to create. When we share these models, we can attract the elements needed to make them real.

AFFIRMING INTENTIONS
THROUGH A PLEDGE OR PROMISE

Everyone has made a promise to himself or herself or to another person, and we certainly have done so as citizens of the United States. We are asked, as students, to pledge allegiance to our country. When we promise something or pledge, it is an affirmation. It is an affirmation with some power behind it because it indicates a commitment. We say, "I promise you that I will do this" or "I will work on this" or "I will make this happen" or "I will be there for you." It's a very strong statement especially for people who believe that their word is their bond, who walk their talk, and who try faithfully to live up to their promises.

External events can make it difficult for us to adhere to our promises. There is an expectation that when you say "I pledge" or "I promise" that you are going to do everything within your power to transform your intention into reality. A promise or pledge is really an affirmation with some extra energy behind it.

An affirmation is essentially a promise or vow that you make to yourself about what you plan to do, need to do, or feel should happen. Empowering leaders are people who make and keep promises to themselves. At one level, affirmations are simply that. "I won't behave in this way" or "I will create this action." Those are essentially promises that you are making.

Vows are even stronger than promises. If you state your intentions as vows they are less likely to become empty statements. The character of Stuart Smalley on *Saturday Night Live* used to say, "I'm good enough, and I'm smart enough, and gosh darn it, people like me." It's a funny bit because there's a sense that he doesn't really mean it but is still mouthing the affirmation without having a strong intention and belief behind it.

Your intention and belief empowers your promise. Empty affirmations are useless. The only way they are not empty is if you put some *oomph* behind them, and the *oomph* is your commitment to making them real.

REPETITION CAN BE A USEFUL FORM OF AFFIRMATION

As a rule of thumb, when making an affirmation, it is best to repeat it three times in succession. For example, "I am healthy and energetic." "I am healthy and energetic." "I am healthy and energetic." The more you repeat something, the more concrete it becomes. In education and in advertising, we know that it takes repetition to break through the noise and set ideas in our mind. Sustained repetition over time embeds our affirmations in both the conscious and unconscious aspects of our mind. When affirmations become internalized, the power intensifies.

It is important to remember that this is all voluntary. We're not compelled to have an affirmation or to repeat it. It is something that we choose to do. Increasing the frequency of an affirmation increases its power. It's like forming a good habit. The more we practice the desired behavior, the better we become at it. Affirmations can help you to create habits that are positive and empowering.

Affirmations can be used in all aspects of our lives. They work best when stated as though they are already true. For example, suppose you want to lose ten pounds. Instead of stating your intention is to drop from 180 pounds to 170 pounds, your affirmation might be this: I weigh 170 pounds and feel really good. Saying this aloud three times in succession, three times a day increases the likelihood that you will achieve your intention.

If possible, do one of the sequences while looking at yourself in the mirror. This will help incorporate your affirmation into the unconscious aspect of your mind. This works because our unconscious mind believes what we tell it. It is not judgmental like our conscious mind. Our unconscious mind works to align our reality with the messages we give it.

The affirmation process, which only takes a minute or two, can be used to incorporate the core values that we are writing about in this book into the way you lead as an empowering leader. Whatever it is you are trying to bring into your life or to accomplish, in terms of who you are and what you want to do, using affirmations increases the likelihood that it will happen.

CREATING A SECULAR MANTRA

Originally, a mantra was a word, sound, or phrase uttered repeatedly that is associated with a Buddhist or Hindu deity. In secular use it has come to mean a slogan or statement that is repeated frequently. From that perspective an affirmation can be viewed as a secular mantra.

Dr. Herbert Benson, a professor of mind/body medicine at Harvard Medical School, wrote *The Relaxation Response*. In it he suggests that we can select a word or phrase that has meaning for us and use it as a mantra.

Statements such as, "I'm here to be of service to my fellow man," or "Black lives matter," or "We can create a better world," or "I'm healthy and happy," can all be used as mantras. We just have to say it over and over. Benson showed that mantras trigger a relaxation response. While this is certainly true we believe they can do even more. It is our view that mantras can be used for good or ill. Empowering leaders use them for their own well-being but also in the service of others.

In the movie *Wall Street*, Gordon Gekko's mantra was "Greed is good." He used that mantra repeatedly, and it was certainly effective. It may have been empowering to him, but, clearly, it was not used in the service of others or the common good. Mantras and affirmations are powerful tools, but we are always responsible for how we use our power.

In some ways, secular mantras are wish-fulfilling processes. We've all heard the phrase "Be careful what you wish for." Some people wish for things that may not be good for them, and they will have to deal with the consequences of their choices. Gordon Gekko chose the three words: "Greed is good." The movie wouldn't have been as interesting, but he could have chosen "Service is good" or "Kindness is good" or "Love is good." You can create any secular mantra you want. Affirmations don't have to be original; you are only limited by your imagination. As an empowering leader, we advocate choosing mantras that make you and your organization better.

CREATING A PERSONAL MISSION
STATEMENT IS A USEFUL FORM OF AFFIRMATION

A personal mission statement, for those of us who might be willing to write one, is in essence the road map for our life, laying out in an affirmative way where we want to go and what we want to be about. Stephen Covey, in his book, *7 Habits of Highly Effective People,* recommended that we create personal mission statements. He suggested that people review them from time to time to see if the way their life is unfolding is in accord with their personal mission statement. Mission statements are usually grand in scope. Affirmations have a narrower focus. For example, a personal mission statement might be like this: *To make the world better by teaching core principles of empowering leadership.* Whereas, an affirmation might be this: *I conduct workshops on empowering leadership with skill and effectiveness.*

All you have to do to change this personal mission statement into an affirmation is to change the word *to* into an *I.* The personal mission statement recrafted as an affirmation would be this: *I make the world better by teaching core principles of empowering leadership.*

Most leaders are familiar with crafting mission statements for their organization, where naturally the organization is in focus. A personal mission statement puts you, the leader, in focus. It's about who you are and what drives you. You can then change it to an affirmation by changing the thrust from the future to the present.

It is a bit paradoxical because you are writing about what you envision for the future as though it is already a reality. Instead of saying, "I will make the world better" or "I intend to make the world better," you say, "I make the world better." In effect you are affirming that you, in fact, make the world better. That's what transforms your statement into an affirmation.

A personal mission statement is personal, not in the sense that you keep it private, although you can, but it is personal in the sense that it is individualized. Recrafting it as an affirmation is a technique that helps you express who you are and what is central to the way you see yourself actually manifesting a new reality.

SWEARING AN OATH IS A
POWERFUL FORM OF AFFIRMATION

The notion of an oath has a sense of finality to it. It's more than a promise. It's more than a prayer. It's putting everything on the line. History is replete with stories about people who have sworn an oath of allegiance, or an oath of service, or an oath of revenge, or whatever else the oath was about.

In the movie *Braveheart*, William Wallace, played by Mel Gibson, swears an oath to fight to the death to defend Scotland against the invading English soldiers. In the TV series *Game of Thrones*, the main characters continually declare their fealty in the form of an oath to one lord or another as alliances and power shifts.

Oaths can be positive or negative. Some oaths are taken to pledge loyalty to dark forces, like Lord Voldemort in the Harry Potter books, or in satanic worship. An oath connotes a powerful commitment. You are laying it all on the line when you swear an oath, if you mean it.

The Bible, in both the old and new testaments, is replete with references to oaths, vows, and swearing. There are numerous oaths sworn by man to God and by God to man. Oaths were seen as a verbal binding contract of the highest form. Even in modern times, in many courts of law, we put our hands on the Bible and swear an oath to tell the whole truth and nothing but the truth. We have codified in our legal system the power of a sworn oath, and false swearing while under oath is a punishable offense.

Elected officials at all levels of government take an oath while being sworn in to their respective offices from school board members to the president of the United States. Oaths are given in many organizations, including the FBI, CIA, and the military.

We take oaths to abide by certain rules of conduct, to uphold the Constitution and the laws of the nation. Oaths, both written and verbal, represent a commitment to certain truths, actions and values. Oaths have been part of humankind's story through the ages, and stand as the ultimate form of affirmation.

TO BECOME A MORE EMPOWERING LEADER

- See affirmation as an important core value.
- Know that saying affirmations silently can be useful.
- Know that saying affirmations aloud can be useful.
- Use writing and other visual arts in affirmations.
- Affirm your intentions with pledges and promises.
- Use repetition to reinforce and strengthen affirmations.
- Create a secular mantra.
- Create a personal mission statement in the form of an affirmation.
- Recognize oaths as a powerful form of affirmation.

Core Value 4

Having a Sense of Mission or Purpose

A SENSE OF MISSION OR PURPOSE CAN DRIVE US TOWARD OUR BEST DESTINY

Having a sense of purpose drives us toward our best destiny. Having a clear connection to your purpose gathers energy that can be focused on the outcomes. We all have many potential destinies, but there should be one that is most appropriate for each of us. We have many choices we can make in life, but there are certain ones that lead us to the place we need to be.

This is based on our talents and the opportunities that come into our life. Having a clear sense of purpose drives you toward the destiny that is best for you. Empowering leaders have a sense of service to others. This drives them toward leadership roles. Their talents and the various opportunities they have allow them to move to higher levels of leadership and service.

There are different levels of leadership and different roles of leadership. You can see yourself as helping others or helping an organization or healing the world. Spending one's life as an educator is in reality being a leader, and a leader must also be an educator. Leadership is getting work done through others, and this can only happen when the leader becomes the teacher. Empowering leaders are also doctors because they have the role of healing their organizations.

One of the best compliments a leader can hear is that it is obvious that he or she is not just playing the role of leader but are making a difference in their organization. Getting the job isn't the destination. The job is just a vehicle for making things happen. At its core, our mission is to do something and our destiny is to make a difference.

Jobs and titles are simply labels. They do not speak to purpose. Our jobs are not our mission. It is up to each of us to make our purpose evident. It has been said that there is a difference between making a living and making a life. For empowering leaders, it is about making a life of service to others.

Every action we take in life results in an exchange. The question for an empowering leader to ask is whether that exchange is additive or subtractive. Are we adding to the world, or are we taking away? Empowering leaders must see their role in life as creating a more positive world.

Empowering leaders must go beyond discovering their own purpose. They must help those around them discover their own purpose. Finding our purpose creates a sense of joy. We find happiness and feel fulfilled. If we are fulfilling our destiny, we know it in our heart. We can't do what someone else thinks is a wonderful mission for us. It has to spring from our own heart. This is the gift we should aspire to offer to those who work with us and for us.

Sometimes we need others to help us see our own mission. We don't always see ourselves as clearly as others see us. When they help us see our own possibilities, it can be very powerful if it resonates with what is in our hearts. We have all seen people who were given their mission by someone else—a teacher, a parent, a spouse—but if that mission is not resonant with their heart, it usually leads to unhappiness.

However, helping people "find themselves" can be powerful when that discovery aligns with their own deepest sense of purpose. Empowering leaders try to discover what is in the hearts of those they work with and then help guide them toward that purpose.

WE EACH HAVE A SPECIAL ROLE THAT
CONTRIBUTES TO THE WHOLE OF LIFE

There is a dance of destiny that we each undertake. We usually start with an unclear sense of what our role may be, but it becomes pretty obvious early on that we each have different talents, ideas, and attitudes. These all shape what we become.

Some of us are optimists. There are others who have a more pessimistic worldview. Yet, it is very useful for optimists to have some pessimists around because they help constrain the optimist's actions and shape a more realistic approach to problems. The world is full of possibility and disaster, and taking both into consideration is useful if you are a leader.

But it is also good to remember a description of Nelson Mandela that a young South African once made: "You know there are people in the world who see the glass as half full and there are those who see the glass as half empty. And a few, like Mandela, just try to fill the glass." So optimists—

those half-full people—are valuable, and the half-empty people are also valuable, but ultimately, the real role of any leader is to fill the glass.

Some might say that the talents, attitudes, and beliefs we have are simply an accident of nature while others might feel they are predestined from a divine plan. We would argue that no matter how we live our lives, given our predispositions, we would always end up in some role that involved leading, healing, and teaching. So for us, it matters little where we think these roles emanate; what matters is that they are the crucial ones that affect our lives.

An example of a divine plan, or at least a hidden order in the universe, can be found in James Gleick's book *Chaos*, where he describes the Chaos Game. In the game, you start with a rectangle of any size. You then select three of the four sides. Divide those sides in thirds and place the numbers one through six on those points. You can then draw a dot anywhere inside the rectangle. Now you roll the die. Whatever number randomly comes up is used next.

Let's say it is a six. From the point on the side of the rectangle where the six is located to the point you randomly placed inside the rectangle you put a new point—call it A—that is halfway along a line that would connect the six with Point A. This gives you a new point; call it B. Now you roll the die again. Let's say a two comes up. From point two on the rectangle again you find the halfway point between it and Point B. Call the new point C. You continue this process for at least 100 throws of the die. What emerges from this process is astonishing. After several hundred or thousand iterations of this process, the points, like pixels, form a picture of a fern leaf. It doesn't matter how many times you try the process, changing the sequence of the numbers on the rectangle or the size of the rectangle, each time, with the random direction of the die, you still end with a picture of a fern leaf. It appears that there are patterns in nature and in our lives that unfold regardless of the choices made.

Gleick's description of the Chaos Game created by Michael Barnsley will only work if you have a die, a rectangle, and numbers one through six. But when the right circumstances are present, the inherent pattern will always unfold.

We are each a strand in the tapestry of life or a part of the puzzle of life, and the discovery of our purpose is the discovery of which strand or puzzle piece we are. If any strand or puzzle piece is missing, the whole will not be complete. This requires us to think holistically rather than hierarchically.

LeBron James may be a better basketball player and Barack Obama a more gifted politician, but it doesn't mean they are inherently better as human beings than we are. If we view the world hierarchically, there will always be someone more important, more talented, or more powerful than we are. In a more holistic worldview, each of us has a critical value and the opportunity and capacity to contribute in unique ways.

It is difficult for leaders to move away from hierarchical thinking because they owe their perceived power and importance to the hierarchy of which they are part. If you can't be bigger and better because of your role, what's the point? This is the seduction of thinking that your role is you. People at the top of the pyramid are not better or more important than those at the bottom.

If a CEO of a major corporation is crossing a street and doesn't see a truck coming at him and is pulled to safety by a homeless man, who is more important? Well, at that moment, the homeless man is pretty important to that CEO. The CEO's title, salary, and stock options wouldn't mean much after being squashed by a truck. The world is a much more level playing field than we have come to believe, with each life having value and promise. We are not so special because we are all human beings representing one strand or one point in a larger picture. Yet we are each very special because the picture is not complete without us. This is the paradox of mutuality.

The task of an empowering leader is to be on the search for the potential specialness in everyone. One of the authors was once misdiagnosed by a doctor for a problem he had. A pharmacist figured out the problem and set him on the path to recovery. The problem left untreated or mistreated would have resulted in blindness. Who was more important at that point, the highly trained but incorrect medical doctor or the less trained but insightful pharmacist? Empowering leaders must see the specialness in others regardless of their formal title or training.

THE LIGHT OF EMPOWERING LEADERS HELPS OTHERS TO SEE THEIR MISSION OR PURPOSE

It is central to empowering leaders to see others' potential and help them see it as well. This, while empowering, may not always be greeted with gratitude. People fall into their ruts and become very comfortable with what they see as their niche. When someone else comes along and points out their greater possibilities, it can make them uncomfortable.

If you decide you aren't good at something or that you are doing things fine without putting in more effort and someone comes along and tells you that you have greater potential, you might just want them to shut up.

Take the example of someone who thinks that they aren't good at math. They think that they probably have a genetic predisposition against being good at math. They come to embrace their weakness. They will actually brag about how bad they are at math. What happens when someone comes along and tells them they are wrong? They have just completed a project that involved pretty complicated math, so they must be good at math. Now what do they do? They are confronted by the dilemma of dealing with something they have been able to write off before now being a viable option for them. Some people will celebrate this discovery. They will see a new door opened for them. Others have no interest in walking through that door, but it is very rewarding for a leader to point out those doors and help people walk through them. That is the real sense of empowerment.

The problem leaders face is that every gift poses an obligation. In biblical terms, it is seen as "to whom much is given, much is required." When the gift is there it must be recognized and nurtured. Polishing your gifts requires hard work.

One of the greatest powers leaders have is not their positional authority but the fact they hold the high ground and have a perspective not shared by others in the organization. They can make connections others cannot because they can see how the pieces fit. One of the obligations of a leader is to use that high ground to shine a light that allows others to see themselves in a new light and with a new perspective.

A SENSE OF MISSION OR PURPOSE HELPS US TO STAY THE COURSE THROUGH HARD TIMES

Have you ever been in your car, listening to the radio, and you hear a song you like come on, but then the station starts to fade and you get static instead of music? What do you do? Do you get frustrated and change the channels, or do you still try to listen to your song, even if it is fading in and out? If you stay with the station, you are going to hear bits and parts of the song that you really like and that will remind you of the whole song. If you change channels, you miss that feeling. You can hear a song clearly on a different channel that you may not even like. Having a sense of mission helps us get through the static in our own lives. If you really care about what you are doing, you will stick with it. If you don't, then you will decide any song will do.

Here is another way at looking at this: When you are sailing a boat or flying in a plane, you will sometimes hit a patch of bad weather. You have to find a way around the hazard, but that shouldn't cause you to decide on a different destination. Storms do not last forever and are not infinite. There are ways around them. If you can remember where you are going, you can work around life's vicissitudes. Remembering where you are headed can give you the determination and energy to get through tough times.

One way of looking at this is that a leader must have "wobbly steadiness." It is like watching an ant crossing the yard in pursuit of a picnic basket. He may encounter rocks and plants that get in the way, but if you trace his path, you would find it *zigging* and *zagging*, but you would also see that he is on course toward the basket. His destination is clear. If you have a sense of mission, you are willing to put up with the obstacles in your path and can get to where you need to go.

A SENSE OF MISSION OR PURPOSE
HELPS US TO TAKE THE LONG VIEW

Purpose isn't simply deciding that you want an ice cream cone. That might be a short-term goal, but it isn't your purpose. Mission and purpose are built over a life's work. You might see it as your journey, which really has no ultimate destination. In our life, we don't really want to get to the end. We just want to keep progressing in the direction of our heart's desire.

When you see your purpose as having a life's worth of pursuit, it is easier to face the day-to-day distractions. While watching a rodeo, one leader saw a young man mount a bucking bronco and try to stay on. His particular journey on this horse was short-lived. Just after he was bucked off, the announcer mumbled into the mike, "It ain't always wonderful." It sure isn't. Sometimes you spend most of your time flying through the air and landing on your behind, but that makes those days when you ride the beast all the more fulfilling.

We are all familiar with the notion of two steps forward and one step back. Sometimes it is two steps back and one step forward, and some days you are just stepping in it! It is important to have a sense of purpose and to take the long view or else life can sometimes seem unbearable.

Think of a coin. It has two sides. One is purpose; the other is a long view. You can't have a successful purpose without taking the long view, and having a long view helps you clarify your mission. In his Nobel Prize acceptance speech, William Faulkner observed that he believed that man would not only endure, but he would prevail. Having a long view allows you to endure. Having a mission or purpose allows you to prevail.

You have to endure to prevail. But simply enduring isn't prevailing. A sense of purpose leads you toward prevailing. You can't prevail without enduring, but simply enduring without the hope of prevailing is merely torture.

Empowering leaders must have a sense of perseverance, patience, persistence, determination, and commitment. But they must also have a sense of forgiveness because you cannot ultimately endure and prevail unless you can get past the problems you have faced and the problems that others cause you.

It is important to have a sense of making progress. It is important for leaders to look forward, but they must also sometimes look back to see where they have been. This peek back allows you to see where you came from and how far you have progressed. You don't have to dwell on the past and spend a lot of time celebrating your victories, but you do need to know how far you've moved to allow yourself the willingness to continue enduring.

EMPOWERING LEADERS ARE AGENTS OF A HIGHER PURPOSE

We all have to decide what team we want to play for. We can align ourselves with a higher purpose, or we can simply align ourselves with our baser instincts. We are not compelled to do something with a higher purpose. It is totally acceptable to do things for ourselves. We just need to understand that will likely limit our ultimate success. We can have the purpose of getting rich or helping others. One serves a higher purpose than the other. Of course, it's possible to have a purpose of getting rich and helping others, which is like having your cake and eating it too.

Knowing we have a choice is incredibly powerful. We are all free agents. When you choose to follow your own purpose, it is very empowering for you. Allowing those who work with you to have a sense of following their own purpose is empowering for them. This can be done within the context of an organization. If the organization has a clear purpose and one aligned to a higher purpose, it frees those within it to do their best work.

When you accept that you are doing something because you choose to do it rather than because you are forced to do it, it is very empowering. It is likely doing the same things, but the power of knowing it is your choice is liberating. Are you simply catering to the base egos of those around you or are you serving a greater purpose? When you decide you are serving something larger than yourself, the work you do becomes much lighter.

There is a story about a man walking through the woods during the middle ages. He sees a great construction site and many men at work. He approaches a man and asks him what he is doing, and the man tells him he is carving stone. Well, that was obvious, so he approaches another worker and asks what he is doing. He tells him he is carving stone to build a building. Not satisfied, the gentleman goes to another worker and asks him what he is doing. He replies that he is carving stone to build a building, and then he adds that the building they are constructing will be a cathedral where for centuries to come people can worship God and seek their higher purpose.

Each of these workers was doing exactly the same work, but their visions for their mission were very different. We must all ask ourselves if we are carving stone or building a cathedral. Are we serving ourselves or a higher purpose?

The real choice we must all make is to decide if we are primarily serving ourselves or others. Are we serving the positive forces in the universe or the baser forces? If we choose the greater good, then we have chosen to be an instrument for something far larger than ourselves. Are we merely breaking rocks or building something lasting?

EMPOWERING LEADERS ARE
SUPPORTED BY THE UNIVERSE

The first decision you must make as an empowering leader is the decision between attunement and alignment. When you are aligned with the universe, things go smoother. There is less friction. The path is smooth. It's like being on rails and you are in sync with what's happening. This allows you to maximize your effort because you are moving easily towards a clear end.

But there is an even better way to approach the world; that is, to gather all your power by being attuned with the universe. You aren't merely moving to an end the universe supports; you are in tune with the purpose of the universe.

When this happens, you can benefit from synchronicity and serendipity. Things just happen to benefit your work. It is almost like magic—the right people show up and help appears. This is the universe supplying what you need. When a leader does the right things for the right reason, in time, opposition melts away and good things happen.

We can see this as "luck," or we can see it as the universe supporting us. Think of all the times in your life you met someone who became important to you. What if you had decided to be in a different place that day? What if you had gone left instead of right? If you think that everything that happens is random and there is no pattern, you will not see the help when it appears and you will be very much alone. If you can accept we are all part of the greater tapestry, a part of the pattern, you can accept the universe's help when it shows up.

MANIFESTING OUR HIGHEST POTENTIAL

Being an empowering leader is accepting doubt in your life. We are all familiar with people who seem to think they have all the answers and who exhibit no doubt. You might argue that lacking self-doubt is delusional. None of us really know what life will bring. There is an old joke that suggests that if you want to make God laugh, tell him you have a plan.

Life is made up of vicissitudes and surprises. As the comic character Rose-anne Rosannadanna used to observe, "It just goes to show you. It's always something. If it's not one thing, it's another." Life is that something else and you never know what's going to unfold.

Now this can depress you and make you wonder what the point is, or you can choose to have a point and move forward. If you believe you have a higher purpose, you can seek help in moving toward it. One of the interesting things about potential is that none of us ever reaches it. Chances are even Einstein didn't use all his brain. In all likelihood, there were days when he got up and wondered if it was worth the bother.

Even the highest achievers never fully reach their full potential. None of us do! Potential is always much greater than the outcome. Knowing this can be a bit frightening and wonderful at the same time. We are all underachievers. So figuring out how to manifest your highest potential is your ultimate challenge.

We are all multidimensional. This allows us to move in the direction where our greatest gifts lie. Leaders must use their leadership potential, but this involves using their potential to focus, to work with others, to forgive, and to empower.

In every field there are world-class exemplars. There is a childhood rhyme that goes, "Good, better, best. Never let it rest, until the good is better and the better is best." The journey of our life should always be toward reaching for the highest potential we have and finding ways to manifest it.

We can fall into a trap of thinking that achievement is about great athletes or entertainers. Most of us don't have talents to be world-class athletes or Oscar-winning actors. But there are millions of things that can and need to be done in this world, and all of us have talents we haven't yet tapped. Talents can be connected to our heart and soul. They can be connected to reaching out to others.

Unfortunately, our society tends to place a value on fame and fortune. This is superficial. Empowering leaders help people see there is much more to life than what shows up in the paper or on the television. Empowering leaders help people see their potential and help them manifest it.

Our potential is virtually limitless. As long as we have imagination and a willingness to work, we can manifest greatness. The standard for greatness varies with each of us. We might be the greatest sculptor or we might be the greatest stone worker. If we can tie our potential to our mission and purpose, we can make the world a better place. Empowering leaders should constantly focus on better understanding their mission and purpose and tying that to the purpose and potential of those around them.

EMPOWERING LEADERS

- Allow their purpose to drive them toward their best destiny.
- Understand that we each have a special role that contributes to the whole of life.
- Use their light to help others see their mission or purpose.
- Understand that a sense of mission or purpose helps us stay the course through hard times.
- Know that a sense of mission or purpose helps us take the long view.
- Know we are free agents of a higher purpose.
- Believe the universe supports them.
- Help us manifest our highest potential.

Core Value 5

Learning to Balance the
Head and Heart

Empowering leaders are leaders who have a strong sense of their work, how it can be improved, and most important, how they can help those around them be more efficient and effective. They have the skills and knowledge to lead. However, if a leader does not operate from an open heart, the "head" part of their work will be for naught. Often, it is hard for a leader to acknowledge that the heart has any place in leadership. When you are driven by results and outcomes, they tend to push out what some consider the softer side of leadership. This leads us to allow our head to fight with our heart or to ignore its rightful place in our leadership. We know we need to do something, but we feel that another course is the right one. Empowering leaders operate from the value of balancing what is in their heads and in their hearts. They take their knowing and their feeling into consideration.

There is a story about an old Native American grandfather who is advising his grandson. He tells him that he has two wolves fighting within him. One wolf is an evil wolf and is full of anger, hatred, greed, bitterness and envy. The other wolf is a good wolf and is full of love, compassion, trust, hope, optimism and forgiveness. He tells his grandson that the same battle is taking place within him also. The grandson is alarmed and asks his grandfather which wolf will win. The grandfather replies that it is the wolf that we feed. We tend to feed one part of ourselves at the expense of the others.

LEARNING TO FEED THE HEAD AND THE HEART

We all have internal conflicts between our lower instincts and our better angels, such as in the case of the two wolves in the story. Often they are merely a struggle between our knowing and our feeling. Whenever there is internal conflict, a leader becomes immobilized. It is hard to act when the direction is unclear. It becomes critical that the leader learn to understand these internal conflicts and to learn to find balance between them. When we lean too far toward our head, the world becomes objectified and intellectualized. The head is useful for analyzing and putting things together, but the head isn't very useful in understanding and acting on feelings and emotions.

The very act of leadership is dealing with other humans, who are a collection of life experiences, hopes, traumas, desires, and dreams. Empowering leaders must understand the power of emotions and empathize with those they lead at the level of spirit. The heart is the gateway for understanding the spirit of another. However, you can't only work from the heart because you will miss the bigger picture and the context of your decisions. It is not a matter of *either/or* but a matter of *and.* It is the head *and* the heart that are the prime tools in a leader's toolbox.

Those in an organization know if a leader is imbalanced. They can tell if a leader is operating solely from the head. Head leaders emphasize data and outcomes. Heart leaders emphasize feelings and morale. Empowering leaders emphasize both to achieve long-term success. They try to find the balance that allows the organization to succeed so that those in the organization feel a sense of ownership and accomplishment.

In today's world, where outcomes seem to trump every other matrix, it is difficult for the heart to find its place in the leader's world. However, leaders who drive an organization toward excellence without understanding the power of the heart tend to use up their people. Their organizations are marked by low morale and high turnover. The heart provides the path to renewal and regeneration in an organization just as the head provides the clear roadmap and motivation for success.

It is crucial for a leader to be clear-headed, but an empowering leader is also clear-hearted. Clear-headed people see clearly and clear-hearted people feel clearly. Both are required to truly be an empowering leader. Clear-headed leaders see the way forward in ways that allow those around them to understand so they can align themselves around the goals. A clear-hearted leader feels things in such a way that creates emotional resonance with those around him so that they want to align with the goals.

AVOIDING THE DANGER OF IMBALANCE

The dangers of working only from the head are clear. There is a tendency to ignore what is happening to the people in the organization. There are also dangers from working only from the heart. The heart is driven by emotion, and emotions can create static in the head so that movement is stymied. We say that these people are not thinking clearly, and they aren't.

A person we know once attended a funeral of someone who he had known slightly. He then went back to the home of the grieving family to share his condolences. The daughter-in-law of the deceased commented that, even though he hadn't known the family well what he had done was important and appreciated. The author replied that he always tried to do the right thing. He was responding to her heart observation with a very heady response. He was applying his judgment as to what was right or wrong instead of merely feeling what the right response was.

There are times when it is appropriate to respond from the head and times when the heart should drive us. It is important to do both at the appropriate time and place. In biblical terms, "To everything there is a season." Empowering leaders understand the seasons and adapt appropriately. If someone from the organization is hurting, a head response is not appropriate. If someone needs concrete direction, responding with a feeling or an emotion will probably leave them feeling lost and untethered.

We have witnessed some of our presidents at their best moments when they have led a grieving nation with strong but soothing words. Presidents have been called the "Mourner in Chief" for these sorts of moments. And sometimes they elevate us to a higher place by transforming our grief into action. That is head and heart leadership at its best.

The simple truth is that when we become unbalanced, we fall over. That is true literally and figuratively. Head only leaders can do great analysis and problem solving but they can't seem to enlist their followers in taking action. Using only the heart leaves solutions to problems on the table and the problems continue.

LEADERS MUST INTEGRATE
THE HEAD AND THE HEART

The first requirement for integrating the head and the heart is to accept that it is necessary. As we have already pointed out, many leaders tend to emphasize one over the other—they play to their strength. The other requirement is that a leader must constantly shift between the head and the heart—balance comes from drawing from both. It is almost impossible to work both simultaneously so a constant shifting between them is necessary.

A good metaphor for this is a trip to the optometrist. When checking your vision, he covers one of your eyes and has you look through a lens with the other—then he shifts to another lens and asks you which helps your vision more. Often, it requires a number of shifts back and forth before the correct lens is chosen. This movement back and forth creates an integration and an energy of connection. This is true for working the head and the heart—you have to go back and forth to get the right vision for your work.

It is important to understand that the head and the heart each have a different wisdom for us. When the heart and head are aligned, we can tap into both wisdoms. The challenge for an empowering leader is to sort through the signals he is getting from his head and his heart and to find the common ground between them.

When one of us was a superintendent, there was a struggle to get the high school graduation speeches just right. The graduates are having a big night and mostly want to be entertained. For them, it is all about the emotion of the moment. The parents and grandparents see graduation as a seminal event for their children and are looking for conveyed wisdom. Writing a speech that combines both requires drawing on the head for the wisdom and the heart for the connection to a bunch of celebratory eighteen-year-olds.

One year, the superintendent had a graduating senior murdered the day before graduation. He had to scrap his prepared speech and try to offer solace to a traumatized community. In his speech, he pointed out there are times when the heart must understand what the mind cannot comprehend. That is offering the idea of balance between the heart and the head. Comprehension is a head activity. Understanding comes from the heart. The mind requires a logic the heart does not recognize.

There are some things that happen in our lives that the head will never comprehend. It requires the heart to provide the balm for that. There was a wonderful quote from the Greek writer Aeschylus that Robert F. Kennedy used in a speech to a grieving audience the night Martin Luther King Jr. was killed. Aeschylus wrote that "he who learns must suffer. And even in our sleep, pain that cannot forget, falls drop by drop upon the heart, and in our own despair, against our will, wisdom comes to us by the awful grace of God." That is the wisdom the heart can show us. There are times when a leader must speak directly from the heart because the head, in those moments, is inadequate and inappropriate for the task.

All of us have witnessed leaders speaking. Which are the most effective— the ones who slave through a prepared text to make certain that every idea is given full hearing, or the ones who speak directly to the audience using eye contact and human connection? The answer is obvious. One is stilted and off-putting. The other feels spontaneous and authentic in a way that connects to the other person.

Throughout our work, we have used the notion of *integrity* as a core value for an empowering leader. That is because someone who has integrity has been able to integrate their head and their heart to weave together what they say with what they do. Authenticity is obvious to all. So is inauthenticity.

We know someone who has always used metaphors in his speaking and writing. In part, this is because he was raised in a rural setting by a minister father. He couldn't escape the influence. There is a reason religious leaders have used story and parable as a teaching tool. But the use of metaphor for a leader is also powerful because it provides a linkage between the head and the heart. Listeners can understand better the concept they have been given, and they can feel it from the picture the metaphor offers. Part of a metaphor is intellectual and part is emotional. When you can combine both, it is a powerful way of stating your case.

EMPOWERING LEADERS MUST BE
AFFECTIVE AS WELL AS EFFECTIVE

Affective leaders lead from the heart. They care about the people they serve and they connect at a human level. Effective leaders care about the organizations they serve and they connect at an intellectual level. One is not preferable over another. Both are necessary to supercharge an organization and its people. Empowering leaders must be effective by knowing and doing the right things, but they should also be affective by feeling and touching others' hearts in the right way.

We would argue that it is not possible to be an effective leader without being an affective one and vice versa. Each facilitates the other. Touching another person profoundly comes through affective acts. This helps build loyalty and good connections between people that leads to more effective work on their part. Effective leadership provides the direction; affective leadership provides the bonds that tie the organization together and give the impetus to reach the goal.

An interesting example of this is former mayor of New York, Rudy Giuliani. For seven-and-one-half years, he was, by all accounts, an effective mayor. He cleaned up the city, lowered the crime rate, and balanced the budget. He didn't win a lot of friends in the process because his leadership style was controversial and he more closely resembled a bull in a china shop than a prima ballerina. He knew the right things to do as a mayor and he forged ahead doing them without much consideration for what others might think or feel. The last half-year of his time as mayor saw him become a very different type of leader.

When the Twin Towers fell, he became an *affective* leader. He helped his community understand what their minds could not comprehend. He comforted grieving families and assured a city it would emerge stronger than ever. He was able to say the right things, do the right things at the right time, take the right actions, and be in the right places with a real sense of authenticity that buoyed people's spirits and helped heal a hurting city. He gave them a sense of hope and optimism. By doing so, he became not just New York's mayor but the world's mayor. And he did that not by putting in new programs or processes but by connecting emotionally. By the end of his term he was both an effective mayor and an affective one.

LEADERS' ACTIONS ARE MAGNIFIED

It is good for leaders to remember that whatever they do gets magnified within their organization. They are under the microscope. What they focus on becomes the focus of others and how they lead becomes the style within the organization. A leader who leads only with the head will have an organization that is long on analysis and results and short on feelings. Likewise, a leader who leads only with the heart will have an organization that sacrifices outcomes for the sake of feelings. Leaders who are both effective and affective will demonstrate balanced priorities to their staff.

LEADERS CAN OVERCOME
THE DOMINANCE OF THE HEAD

The first step in overcoming head dominance is to realize you have a problem. Empowering leaders are open to looking at their leadership style and their values. If it is hard for you to do that, you might want to ask someone you trust in the organization how they see you. (Of course, if there is no one you can trust in the organization, you have a bigger problem than mere head dominance!) For example, going back to another New York mayor, Ed Koch, you might recall he was known for walking up to strangers on the street and asking, "How am I doing?" We are sure he got many polite, noncommittal answers, but knowing New Yorkers, we suspect he also got an earful from time to time. This unvarnished feedback helped him to be a better mayor. He modeled an openness and interest in his constituents, and he became respected and liked by many throughout the city.

If you create a culture of trust and are prepared to be vulnerable to having your weaknesses exposed, you can get feedback from your environment that tells you if your head is too dominant.

One of the weaknesses of our culture is that we tend to think hierarchically. We know the *boss* is over others and we know the head is literally above the heart. Therefore, we start to think that the *boss* knows all and that the head is somehow better than the heart. Neither is true.

Historically, our society has tended to view females as being more "heart" oriented and males as more "head" oriented. Again, that has tended to reinforce a stereotype of the heart that means it shouldn't be used by hard-headed leaders. What we are now seeing in our society is the emergence of highly effective female leaders who have found a balance between their heads and hearts. In many ways, our hierarchical thinking has led us down some wrong roads. One way of getting rid of the dominance of one aspect of our leadership is to understand that dominance, itself, is a problem. Your head and heart are a team, like a pair of dancers or skaters, and both are better because of the collaboration with the other.

As children we often played on the "seesaw." We know that it took both ends, working together, to have a good experience. If one end dominated, it left the other end up in the air, hanging on for dear life. Another example would be piano players, who use both hands, one to provide the harmony, the other to provide the melody. Once you come to accept the need for harmony in your work, you can begin to give up the idea of the dominance of one part of your leadership style.

Another negative trait of our society has led us to have lots of information but little wisdom. The expansion of electronic media has inundated us with information. The problem is sorting through it and making sense of it. In our increasingly complex world, rather than having more answers, we have more questions. To find our wisdom, we must use all our tools and that, for leaders, means using both their head and heart.

A head-dominant leader must work to get in touch with her feelings, but more is needed. Once in touch, she must find ways of expressing her feelings openly to others. This allows those in the organization to see the leader is leading with her heart, as well as her head. You can argue our society is making progress on this front. Some of us remember Senator Ed Muskie being knocked out of the presidential race because he teared up in a speech. Today, it is nearly mandatory that politicians tear up regularly. Former Speaker of the House Boehner is known as a prolific crier. We are not suggesting that a leader has to cry on cue to be effective. But we are suggesting that a legitimate integration of one's heart into his leadership and then having the ability to show that integration is crucial to building an effective organization.

LEADERS CAN OVERCOME THE
DOMINANCE OF THE HEART

A central question for any leader to ask is this: "What do I have to do to be more effective?" For a leader who leads from the head, of course, she needs to learn to lead from the heart. But likewise, a leader who favors the heart needs to learn how to involve the head more. Again, she needs to switch the lens regularly to make sure that her leadership and decisions are not being driven by feelings only. She needs to use some of the tools a head leader uses. She needs to ask herself, "What is the logical thing to do here? Is this a rational approach to our challenge? What is the best judgment I can make at this time?" She needs to learn to apply those "head" words to her leadership process. We know that bad logic can lead to bad decisions, but bad heart logic can lead to bad decisions also.

There is a tendency to view "heart" leaders as being too soft and not having high enough expectations. And when the heart dominates there is real truth to that criticism. Having the ability to integrate the head with the heart allows a natural heart leader to do those things that are sometimes necessary to create success in an organization. One of the things a heart leader must consider is not just what is best for an individual in an organization but what is best for the entire organization, and be balanced in looking at the consequences.

There are certainly times when individual compassion is called for, but if you forget about the impact of that compassion on others, it can hurt the organization. The danger of the head-dominant leader is looking at the forest and forgetting the individual tree, and the danger of the heart-dominant leader is looking at the tree and forgetting the forest. Working from a head perspective, you have to zoom in occasionally on the smaller picture to understand what is happening to individuals in the organization, and working from a heart perspective, you have to pull your lens out and look at the bigger picture from time to time to see the effect on the organization. Doing both creates the balance we need.

What do you do if you are confronted with a situation where someone in your organization has a serious sickness or problem? Can you show compassion without endangering the organization? And if you don't show enough compassion does that also endanger the organization? This is why some organizations allow employees to create sick leave pools where they contribute to the pool for their colleagues who might be facing a serious health crisis so they can draw sick days from the pool once their own are exhausted.

Sometimes compassion must be driven by the context of the person being considered. Have they contributed to the organization and is there a good chance that compassion will make them effective again? Or have their actions proved destructive to others in the organization and will your compassion simply weaken the organization further? These are the kinds of questions a leader must navigate when balancing the head and the heart.

Good leaders carry water on both shoulders. On one shoulder, you are carrying the water of the individual you are considering, and on the other, you are carrying water for all those in the organization. Empowering leaders try to make sure they do not have too much water on one side and not enough on the other. Even though two full buckets are heavier than a full one and an empty one, being able to balance both keeps you from falling over.

LEADERS MUST CREATE A CULTURE WHERE THE HEAD AND THE HEART ARE VALUED

Leaders should understand that their own actions are the loudest statements they can make. They have to create a culture where both head and heart are valued and demonstrate to others they are doing so. They must go further to nurture and reinforce both in others. As leaders are building their teams, they need to make certain that they have head-dominant and heart-dominant members represented. This will create a synergy on the team where both parts are constantly in play.

One of the roles for the leader as he builds a balanced team is to create a tolerance for each style on the team. We both have had teams that were a mixture of head and heart people. When tolerance was present (and it usually isn't present by accident—it must be cultivated), there was a real power to the team that allowed them to be effective and to stand up to outside pressures and challenges. When tolerance was not cultivated, there was a lot of bickering and backbiting.

Creating tolerance is seeing past the outer wrapping to appreciate what was inside the package. A person might appear to be kind of goofy and distracted but often that person is the source of creative ideas. Another might appear to be an uptight rule follower but that person helps ensure things get done and that they happen on time and properly. The source of tolerance on a team comes from seeing past the outside and beyond the often-annoying behaviors that we all exhibit and learning to appreciate the inner strengths that are there. The value is not in the wrapping and ribbon; it is what's inside the box.

An empowering leader makes certain that all perspectives are heard and appreciated. He shows that he has equal respect for those coming from the heart and the head. He shows this by the amount of attention he pays to them, the way he reiterates and repeats some of the points they are making, and the way he shines his light equally on the people coming from both perspectives.

One of us once had a team where one person was often highly emotional and volatile but who had sensitivity for issues from the point of view of justice and ethics. Certain values issues triggered that person's emotion. The one of us who was working with this person was able to recognize that when the "alarm" went off with this person, there was an important perspective being voiced. Even though the message was sometimes uncomfortable or overwrought, with patience and understanding, it was possible to see the deeper wisdom that was being expressed. This calls for a leader not just to build a team with differing styles and values but a leader who also has the insight to pick up what these varied people are bringing to the table and the openness to draw upon it.

Empowering leaders build a culture of acceptance, but they must go further to value and even revere those things that their team members are bringing forward. It takes a lot of different voices to create a choir. You need the tenors, the altos, the sopranos, and the baritones for the music to sound right. A choir of only sopranos can be a bit screechy. A choir of baritones is a little monotonous. Finding the balance and helping them find the harmony within them allows the organization to flourish. A leader who has that internal balance between her own inner voices from the head and heart can be a highly effective conductor.

TO BECOME A MORE EMPOWERING LEADER

- Learn to feed the head and the heart.
- Avoid the dangers of imbalance.
- Learn to integrate the head and the heart.
- Learn to become affective as well as effective.
- Understand that your actions are magnified.
- Learn to overcome the dominance of the head.
- Learn to overcome the dominance of the heart.
- Create a culture where head and heart are valued.

Manifesting Your Vision

LEADERS MUST USE THE POWER OF
THOUGHT TO MANIFEST THEIR VISION

The interesting thing about vision is how many people lack it. Even if they have a sense of a vision, it is often lacking coherence and it is difficult for them to describe their vision to others. Further, in today's self-centered world, far too many individual visions are just that—serving only the individual. The first thing a leader needs to do is develop a personal sense of vision and then help those in the organization develop their individual and joint visions.

The leaders of the Urban Superintendent's Program at Harvard required each of their students to develop a "vision" speech as part of their graduation requirement. They had to spend months honing it and then present it to a very critical audience. This was a very rigorous exercise requiring the students to have clarity about their own values, mission, and hopes for their work. It would be interesting to see how many CEOs might have difficulty with that assignment.

The leader's vision is very personal. It includes his values and goals as a leader, but then leaders need to shape their own personal vision to the one the organization holds for itself. And they must have alignment between their personal vision and that of the organization. In that process, they have to help each person in the organization find their own vision.

If leaders have a hard time describing their vision, it is then nearly impossible for most organizations to describe theirs. The role of a leader is to be able to articulate the vision of the organization in such a way that those in it say, "Yes, that is what we are about." They may never have thought about it consciously, but when they hear it, they know it.

When the personal vision of the leader and the organizational vision are not aligned, conflict ensues. The leader becomes ineffective and the organization becomes dysfunctional. A leader needs to understand and articulate her vision and then understand and articulate the vision of the organization and make certain both are in alignment.

Learning theory says if you increase time on task (the time a student spends directly working on something), student understanding and learning increases. This is also true for organizations. The more time a leader and her organization spend focusing on their vision and what it means for the organization the more that vision becomes manifested in the actions of the organization.

The process works on a number of levels. The first step is the "brainstorming" stage where the ideas around the vision are tossed out and played with. Then, as mental energy is applied, the vision begins to take form. As the various elements of the vision are identified, the vision comes into greater focus until it is crystal clear.

At one level, we use our minds in this process. As our minds work through the process, we are also sending out mental energy around the vision to the greater universe. That is when synchronicities (see bonus chapter 1) begin to happen as that thought energy is returned to the sender with tangible support.

In biblical terms, it is believed that where your treasure is, your heart energy is also, and vice versa. What you value is what surrounds you in life. By focusing on what you value and what you wish to bring into the reality of the organization, that act of treasuring begins to create a reality around you.

Suddenly you begin to discover buried treasure in your organization. When you put your thoughts and mental energy to work, it brings actual possibilities into your world. What you focus on attracts and expands. When this happens your world begins to expand and to flow in the direction of your desire.

The actor Alan Alda, known for playing a doctor on the hit TV series *MASH*, told a group of graduating doctors, "Our head bone really is connected to our heart bone." The power of thought recruits the heart and that amplifies the energy we have to transform our thoughts into reality. This creates passion and energy. Sadly, many organizations go through a planning process that squeezes all the passion juice out of those involved. An empowering leader is aware that the heart must be a central part of any visioning process.

VISUAL IMAGERY CAN BE USED TO
HELP LEADERS MANIFEST THEIR VISION

It is important in the process of developing a vision to find the right visual models or symbols for what we want to manifest. Organizations are forever trying to brand themselves with symbols and phrases. Nike uses a swoosh to connote action which ties in with its motto of "Just Do It." FedEx uses an almost subliminal arrow embedded in the letters FedEx on their trucks to promote the idea that they deliver on time. Apple uses the once-bitten apple to tie into Sir Isaac Newton's discovery of gravity—a company that does new things and is willing to take a bite out of the apple.

Organizational models can be two-dimensional symbols or they can actually be three-dimensional objects. An interesting exercise to try during a visioning process is to ask the team involved to create a three-dimensional object that connotes the vision being developed. This is a way of making a mental model concrete. This helps clarify the vision and begins to create a sense of energy around it.

At the individual level, the process is pretty straightforward. You can have a vision of being healthy and fit. You develop a picture of what you would look like in that state. Maybe you cut out a picture of a very fit person and paste your face on the picture. Then as you move forward and are tempted to eat something you shouldn't you can look at the picture and that will create cognitive dissonance with the vision you have for yourself.

One leader we know had a vision of involving a well-known celebrity in the work of his organization. For several years, every time he saw the celebrity or read about him, he saw the celebrity working with his organization. This powerful image drove the leader's action to focus on ways to meet the celebrity and to find a connection with the work of the celebrity and the leader's organization. Ultimately, this led to an introduction to the celebrity who then was willing to meet with the members of the leader's organization to great effect.

As Cinderella reminds us, "A dream is a wish your heart makes." Having the dreams and wishes for your organization allows you to create opportunities for fulfillment of those dreams.

Having a vision that exists in three dimensions allows you to see it from all sides. This opens new opportunities for making it so. Ultimately, the vision should focus on what your corner of the world would look like once the vision is fulfilled. What would the new product look like? What would happen once it is put out in the world and embraced? What would our organization look like? How would we feel?

THE POWER OF THE SPOKEN WORD CAN HELP LEADERS TO MANIFEST THEIR VISION

Putting words to the vision is adding another layer to it. It is like adding additional senses. The picture or three-dimensional vision appeals to our visual and tactile senses, while words appeal to our hearing. The more senses you employ the more powerful the outcome will be. Putting words to the work sends out a signal of commitment.

The leader we were speaking of who wanted the celebrity involvement in his organization added to the power of this vision by telling everyone he knew that he wanted that person to speak at the organization's annual conference. When you put words to your vision, you are sending a signal that you are serious and you are inviting others to join the enterprise. They can see that what you want connects with what they want as well.

It is often stated that the president of the United States has a "bully pulpit," which allows him or her to share ideas, hopes, and dreams that moves the nation toward those ideas. The truth is we all have bully pulpits, but too often we fail to use them.

The more we talk about those things that are aligned with our vision, the more we increase the energy around it, and the more we gather others to the vision. Again, in biblical terms, some of the first words of the Bible are "Let there be." The pharaohs of ancient Egypt ordered, "So let it be written, so let it be done." The spoken word of "let it be" is the beginning of creating something new for the organization.

As a leader, you are the head of a team of explorers. There is danger in striking out for an unknown world. You never know what you will find. If you are smart, you have guides. They might be mentors, advisors, or your higher powers, and you still might not find what you were looking for.

Lewis and Clark were searching for the Northwest Passage and found half a continent filled with wonders. Columbus was seeking a route to India, but synchronicity helped him find two new continents. Sometimes our original vision must be modified as we discover new things, but we must remain aware it is the original vision that allows the new things to appear.

We have to have a sense of where we want to go and we have to be open to new discoveries along the way. But first, we have to get in the game. Columbus would not have discovered a new world if he sat home on the couch. Setting a vision is the first step away from the couch. There is magical power in the thought of visualizing a new world, but you have to take actions to make it so.

THE POWER OF AFFIRMATION CAN BE
USED TO HELP MANIFEST YOUR VISION

Affirmation provides a focus and discipline for creating a vision. When you have a specific idea that you repeat on a regular basis, it gives you a focus.

You might think of affirmation as the discipline of dreaming. It is the regular creation of energy toward that which you wish to see happen.

Affirmation combines the power of the spoken word and the written word. You can choose whether to memorize your affirmation or to read it. You can also decide whether this is done aloud or silently. You may also choose to share your affirmation with others, which again increases its power.

Affirmations can be used for personal as well as organizational growth and development. The best affirmations are those that describe the reality you intend. You state it as though it already exists. You might say, "I intend to lose ten pounds," but a more powerful way of affirming this is to say, "I see myself ten pounds lighter." You are stating it as though it already exists. In essence, the use of affirmation is creating your own virtual reality. Seeing it as real vastly increases the chances that, ultimately, it turns into reality. You are painting a picture of a scene you intend to visit. When you use affirmation to support your vision for yourself or your organization you are creating the future reality that you want to see. This, again, creates real power and allows you to supercharge your vision of the future. The key is to stay disciplined by repeating the affirmation regularly over time.

The important part of the discipline of using an affirmation is to make certain that you repeat it with thought. You shouldn't just recite the words like a long ago memorized song. Think about what the words mean. When you put out rote energy, you get back rote energy.

We are all familiar with children reciting the Pledge of Allegiance. How many times are they asked to stop and think about what the words mean? Are we really creating a country with "liberty and justice for all"? If so, what would it look like? Do we consider that we can't have liberty without justice, and we can't have justice without liberty? What actions would we need to take to make that real? This would be taking a rote activity and giving it real energy.

When you give off powerful energy, you get back a powerful energy response. As a leader you want to amplify your efforts. You want to connect to your personal power and connect it to the power of others. The sincerity and energy you put into your affirmation amplifies the response you get. You are expanding your own energy. You put out your energy and get it back from all directions.

THE POWER OF PRAYER CAN
HELP MANIFEST YOUR VISION

If you are a believer, you can use prayer as the ultimate way to supercharge your vision. You are appealing to the highest source of support. You are aligning yourself with the greatest source of power in the universe. If you think you are in this all alone, then prayer won't help you much.

However, if you have a sense there is something that you are a part of that is greater than yourself, then sending prayer to that force, spirit or entity, depending on your perspective, enlists that higher power to your aid. You have to triage your prayer. Make sure it is something worth asking for. Praying to win the game isn't really using the process in a meaningful way. Asking to do your best and to serve others is a much better use of your and the universe's time and energy.

The power of prayer increases if it is heartfelt. It isn't your will, per se. It is the alignment of your will with the greater good. It is also important that your prayer be *selfless* rather than *selfish*. It isn't about you. It is about your work in the world.

This whole chapter has been about the power to manifest your vision, but at some point, you have to give in and say, "But on the other hand." Columbus may have prayed to find a new passage to India, but on the other hand he found a new land. Unless you think you are the source of all that is good, you have to be able to let go, and ask that your prayer be in accord with the highest good.

In Joseph Jaworski's book *Synchronicity* (see bonus chapter 1), he describes conversations he had with David Baum in which they discussed the unfolding nature of the universe. When the visions you are trying to manifest are aligned with the unfolding quality of the universe you feel supported and empowered. You feel the flow with the aligned energy. Whether you are seeking help from some divine source or are simply aligning with the universe, you first must ask to be a part of it, then be open to the outcome.

THE POWERS OF SYNCHRONICITY, INTENTION, AND ATTENTION CAN HELP MANIFEST YOUR VISION

The tools of synchronicity, intention, and attention have many uses, but one of them is helping you manifest your vision. You can use synchronicities to help boost the outcome of your vision. You must have the awareness of synchronicities to take advantage of them. You need to recognize them when they show up.

Intention can be used as a form of prayer or as an affirmation. It can help clarify your vision. When your intentions are other focused, you will get more support for them. Attention is attending to what is around you. It is spending the time and energy to allow yourself to be drawn to those things that will support your vision.

Using synchronicity, intention and attention is like having building blocks at your disposal. You are creating something that you can build with and lean on. Empowering leaders want to make things happen. These are a powerful set of tools for doing things for the right reasons.

THE ELEMENTS OF YOUR VISION CAN BE ASSEMBLED IN A NONLINEAR FASHION

Most people tend to view the world in a linear way. A leads to B, which leads to C, but the reality is that the world is very nonlinear. There are patterns, but they aren't always visible or logical. Einstein argued that the world is not random, but few of us have his ability to see the patterns.

It's like going shopping to cook dinner. You have a menu and you determine the ingredients you need for the meal. You go up and down the aisles of the market putting items in your basket. However, sometimes you see something that isn't on your list that gives you an idea for a new course. Again, it is about being open to the possibilities that the universe offers.

You have to be open to the surprises that are out there. If not, you shut off possibilities for a richer outcome. We can't afford to live our lives in a linear fashion while the world operates in such a nonlinear way.

A leader has a vision in mind. It is usually fairly complex and with a lot of elements to it even though some of these are not as clear as others. They are not uniformly defined. A good leader is constantly scanning the universe for artifacts, people, and resources that can be drawn upon to complete the vision. You have to be flexible enough to be open to what shows up and when it shows up. This is the artistic aspect of leadership.

This is not just a creative process; it is an interactive process. Leaders must constantly engage with their environment and pluck things out that will contribute to the holistic vision they have. Life isn't just a puzzle to be solved; it is a canvas to be covered. With a puzzle, you can look at the front of the box to see where everything goes, but a painter has no box to go by.

One of the ironies of life is that there are many paths we can take. But often they go to the same destination. It just takes a little longer to get there with some paths. You can get into trouble thinking there is only one path that is prescribed. You can't just force pieces of the puzzle into place when it is not part of the pattern. Part of the job of living and leading is to catch the flow of events and circumstances and to take advantage of the currents when they are moving in the direction you envision.

MANIFESTING YOUR VISION
THROUGH PARTNERING WITH
PEOPLE AND YOUR HIGHER POWER

As important as we may feel as leaders, the truth is we can't do it alone. It is hard to lead if there is no one available to follow, so we must enlist others in our work. You can try to command them, intimidate them, or coerce them, but it is impossible to bludgeon people to greatness. The most effective thing we can do is partner with them.

When people feel they are partners in the work they feel a share in what happens. They must be a part of developing the vision and creating the tools to make it live. If the vision is powerful enough and good enough the partnering process is contagious as more and more people are brought into the work.

The key is to enlist people. There is a big difference between enlistment and drafting. Drafting is controlled by others and enlisting is a voluntary activity. One is a demand to perform, the other an invitation. Empowering leaders have a sense of power *with* people, not over them.

How you go about partnering makes all the difference. By enlisting, you are inviting people to come along with you toward the vision that is being developed. Far too many leaders operate at the command and control level of behavior. Coercion begets compliance but nothing more. To achieve a higher level of success you cannot lead people with coercive behavior. When you become an empowering leader, you have achieved the highest form of partnering with others.

When you become a true partner with others, you are moving toward a higher form of leadership. You are moving toward a partnership with the higher powers within you and with the universe.

SEE YOUR COMMITMENT TO YOUR VISION
AS A PROMISE TO YOURSELF AND OTHERS

Empowering leadership isn't just about leading an organization; it is about leading others. To be effective you have to be counted upon. This comes from making a commitment to those you lead and serve. You can't expect those who work with you to be committed to you and your collective vision if you aren't committed to their well-being and empowerment.

When you run into problems and challenges, the best thing you can do is recommit to the vision, work, or the relationship. When you commit, you gain a sense of power and energy to move forward.

Most people view commitment as something that takes place over time, but it is really not about length as much as it is about depth. The reality is that no one can say what will happen in the future. All that we have is the present, and full commitment to the work in the present is really all you can promise. It is about getting up each day and recommitting to the vision and the work. This is the promise you can and should make to those around you.

A promise is almost like a contract. It is a mutual obligation you enter into with others. The highest form of integrity a leader can demonstrate is by keeping her word. When the promise is made, it should be seen through.

USE THE ENERGY OF A HIGHER POWER
TO ATTRACT WHAT IS NEEDED TO
MANIFEST YOUR VISION

Whether you are using prayer, meditation, affirmation or intentions, you are attracting energy to manifest your vision. Without drawing upon all the power that is available to you, you are cheating yourself and your organization. It is like a general who tries to fight a battle with an insufficient force, knowing that just over the hill he has thousands of reinforcements, but he refuses to call upon them. He is simply sacrificing his troops by failing to use everything at his disposal.

One way to see how the higher power works is to view it as a laser. It is a focused beam of power that can go over long distances at the speed of light. Another way of seeing it is the tractor beam they had on the television series *Star Trek*. They would use the power of that beam to pull things toward the ship. The energy of a higher power gives you focus over time and can attract things you need to manifest your vision.

All you have to do is ask. You invite it into your life and there it is. You are the vessel or the vehicle for something greater than yourself. Empowering leaders are vehicles of empowerment to those around them. Leadership is the transference of power. The power doesn't belong to the leader. She is not the source of it. She is merely an instrument for passing it on to others.

Leaders are also sometimes the lightning rod of their organizations. They are standing directly in the line of fire, but by channeling the power in the lightning, it can be used for good.

THE WAY YOU VIEW THINGS IS
KEY TO MANIFESTING YOUR VISION

Our way of looking at life will have everything to do with our success in bringing our vision to reality. Do you see the world as a place of peril or possibility? Are you surrounded by light or darkness?

Leaders who see the world as dark or perilous tend to be leaders who limit their work. They think something can't be done because there are so many obstacles to overcome. A leader who sees a world of promise and possibility will ask, "Why not?" The visions these two leaders have will be very different. One will be expansive and the other contracting.

We tend to view things in relation to ourselves and the way they have an impact on us rather than looking at the larger context. The more you see the world through your personal lens, the more difficult it is for you to break out and see a wider world.

Two people can share comparable visions for an organization, but one wants the vision to be successful so they can look good and be a hero while the other is only interested in empowering others and doesn't seek any of the credit. The visions, though similar in intent, will have very different outcomes depending on how expansive the leader is.

Remember the story of the Native American grandfather who tells his grandson that he has two wolves battling within him. One is angry and selfish, while the other is helpful and kind. The grandson is alarmed, and he asks his grandfather which wolf will win. The grandfather replies, "The one you feed."

We all have dark and negative parts of ourselves, and we all have the lighter side. Leaders who feed the wrong wolf within themselves end up being devoured and devouring their organizations. It is incumbent upon the leader to be the most positive voice in the organization and to be the person who brings light to those around him. This is the best way to manifest your vision.

EMPOWERING LEADERS MANIFEST THEIR VISION BY

- Using the power of thought.
- Using the power of visual imagery.
- Using the power of the spoken word.
- Using the power of affirmation.
- Using the power of prayer.
- Using the power of synchronicity, intention, and attention.
- Realizing that the elements of their vision can be assembled in a nonlinear way.
- Partnering with others and their higher power.
- Being committed to their vision as a promise.
- Using the energy of a higher power to attract what is needed.
- Understanding the way that you look at things is key.

Core Value 7

Visualizing Your Way to Success

It has been said that if you don't know where you are going, any road will get you there. Empowering leaders know which roads to take. More important, they know which roads to create for others. They visualize where they want to go with their organizations and then formulate plans and processes to get there successfully. They do this partly by understanding the power of visualization, using symbols, intuition, mental imagery and mental rehearsals of desired outcomes, and meditative techniques.

THE POWER OF VISUALIZATION

We all have countless ideas floating in our head. They can come from almost anywhere: reading, a movie, a television program, an idea pops into our head, or someone makes a suggestion. Certain ideas intrigue us and seem to take root in our mind. We explore some of our ideas by talking and thinking about them and by visualizing various possibilities. At times we see a potential version of reality that strikes us as desirable, something we want to move toward and make real. Visualization is an ongoing process or a series of processes. It is not just a once-and-done process. As we visualize something, we continue to shape and reshape our visualization, particularly if it's something that is complex and multifaceted. We visualize multiple interrelated images. It is like trying to create a movie in your mind's eye about what you want to create, become, or accomplish. This is the first step in manifesting an envisioned reality.

Visualization is a way of authoring your future. It's creating the screenplay from which you will act, or it is the map that you're going to follow. It can be very precise. For example, one of our colleagues remembers using it for a job interview. He visualized the whole process, from the moment he walked into the room and sat down, through the way he conducted himself during the course of the interview, the tone he wanted to set, and the demeanor that he wanted to present. But more than that, he visualized the way he wanted questions to come to him.

He wasn't just creating his response to a given issue. He was creating the issue itself. He also visualized what the other people in the room should be doing. One of the really powerful things he visualized was that when the interview ended, the interviewers wanted to talk more. In his mind's eye the discussion had been so rich that they would have to give him the job in order to continue it. He envisioned a complete scenario with all the roles being played out, not just his. His visualization was more than just planning his actions. He created the whole reality he wanted to manifest. It was a very powerful process. And yes, he did get his dream job.

This colleague, while serving as a superintendent of schools, had a coach who had an extremely successful girls' lacrosse team. The day before each game, this coach would have the team's practice consist of the group sitting down and visualizing the entire game that they were going to play the next day, from beginning to end. They had to visualize the whole team, not just their own actions, passing to other people, receiving from other people, shooting goals, and their defending actions. They sat for about forty-five minutes and went through the whole game in their heads. The kids talked about how powerful that was for them; they always saw themselves winning, of course. With this approach, talent, and good coaching, they won the state championship that year.

Many coaches use similar techniques. There are dancers and other athletes who use this process before their performances. Leadership is a performance art. So why wouldn't it be appropriate for you?

USING SYMBOLS IN A POWERFUL WAY

Empowering leaders can create symbols that are associated with the kinds of things that they're trying to do, both for themselves on an individual basis and for their respective organizations. For example, you could start with a picture that is a symbolic representation of something you want to accomplish. As part of a long-range planning process, a colleague of ours had groups draw pictures of an organization as it existed presently and then draw a picture of that same organization as they envisioned it five years in the future. The picture became a symbol for the aspirational goals and values for those involved in the planning process.

When an organization identifies its core values, it can create symbols to serve as a visual reminder of those shared values. Political leaders are quite adept at this. They wrap themselves in flags. When you associate with a symbol, some of the power that symbol represents transfers over to you.

Artifacts can be used symbolically by empowering leaders. When our colleague, Larry, who is a writer, was in Sedona, Arizona, he purchased an American Indian figurine called a *storyteller*. It is a clay carving of a mother with four children sitting on her lap while she tells them a story. The storyteller sits on his desk in clear view. When he looks at the storyteller, it is a visual symbol that, through the books he writes, he really is a storyteller. Larry also has a couple of feathers in his writing area. One is white and one is black, and they represent the yin and yang or masculine and feminine energy in good storytelling. He has a candle that is symbolic of the light that he is trying to generate through his stories.

A symbol can mean something to Larry and mean something very different to someone else. The key is that it holds meaning for the leader, or for a group of people who have created shared meaning around the symbol. The symbols can be very powerful, whether it's a talisman, or a picture, or a drawing, because it represents something that is much deeper than what we see on the surface. We all need reminders of what it is that we're working to create. Symbols can do that on an individual as well as a collective basis.

Phil Jackson, the former head coach of the Chicago Bulls, had a room in the practice facility where he put certain artifacts. Most of them were Native American, but some were from Eastern religions or from his travels. During the course of the season, he would take the team in the room and talk about why a particular artifact was there, what it represented to him, and what it should mean to them in terms of moving forward with their games that season. He shared the symbols that he had collected to get the players motivated toward certain ends. It is a very powerful way of getting people's attention focused on empowering ideas and values. Phil Jackson used this technique to win eleven NBA championships.

Rachel Raymond shares a similar approach in her book, *My Grandfather's Blessing*, where she describes an activity based on the power of symbols that she uses in retreats. She has a room filled with images and three-dimensional artifacts. They are not really big, but there are lots of them. She encourages the participants to select one or more that they find meaningful. Each person is invited to place the artifacts that they have selected in the center of the room and share what it means to them. People wind up sharing things that are very meaningful to them that usually have a head-heart connection. Other people in the room gain insights, and feel a connection with the members who are participating in a way that had not happened prior to this experience. It is an empowering process.

Our colleague, David, has a collection of Native American fetishes. He sees them as little pieces of art. But in the Native American spiritual tradition, each fetish represents a certain animal, and each animal represents a certain power. Native Americans believe that when you focus on the fetish, you're also focusing on the power of that animal and bringing that power to you. Whether that's true or not may depend on your belief system, but the power of symbols is undeniable. Empowering leaders can create symbols to motivate, build group cohesion, foster team spirit, or create mental pictures for people of desired outcomes for themselves and their organization.

SEEING WITH YOUR "THIRD" OR "INNER EYE"

Depending on your background, having a "third" or "inner eye" is either a familiar or foreign concept. In the West, we usually call it our intuitive sense. In the East, it is often referred to as our "third eye." The "third eye" is depicted as being in the middle of our forehead. A version of it appears on our one-dollar bill at the apex of a pyramid in the form of an "all-seeing eye." For those of you familiar with the body's energy system, rooted in Eastern culture, it is referred to as the sixth chakra used in acupuncture, Reiki, and various meditative traditions. Many people believe, as do we, that our inner eye is a connection to our higher self or divine consciousness. We certainly recognize that this is speculative and not supported by current scientific thinking.

That said, we have found this to be a very useful construct for empowering leaders.

We believe the inner eye connects us to our inner vision, and enables us to connect to the vision that we're trying to create. When David prepared for his interview for superintendent he not only visualized it, but also saw it with his inner eye. The inner eye is able to see through time and space in ways that our physical eyes cannot. We also believe the inner eye sees truth because whatever it sees is whatever is, while the outer eyes can be fooled.

The inner eye has the remarkable property of seeing in both directions. It sees out but it also sees in. It allows us to look inward and draw upon certain aspects of our being and knowing, and it allows us to see out in a way that is clear and true. It is part of the visualization process that we wrote about earlier. We have used the phrase *the mind's eye*. That's another way of saying we can also use our third or inner eye to visualize potentiality or versions of the future. We just don't use our inner eye to look at present reality. We can also use it to look forward to envision possibilities for success.

When you create a visualization with your inner eye, it is solid; it is not distorted. That is why leaders need techniques that can be used to tune into their inner self, whether it's through meditation, yoga, tai chi, prayer, or silence.

In the first decade of the twenty-first century, Peter Senge of MIT was a cofacilitator of a series of dialogues (Call-of-the-Time Dialogue) with leaders from around the globe to promote world peace. In one of their reports, they talked about the power of silence. It was suggested that our ability to see and to know is enhanced remarkably if we will simply create silent space and silent time, to let that inner knowing come through. Our inner knowing comes through our third eye in the form of insight and intuition when we create a space and time for silence. Ask yourself a question, then sit in silence for five to ten minutes and see what your inner eye shows you.

USING MENTAL IMAGERY TO SOLVE PROBLEMS AND SHAPE THE FUTURE

Through mental imagery you can create the solution to a vexing problem. We have a leader friend, who, when he is vexed, starts by sitting down and mentally putting the pieces together that he thinks are needed to build what he wants to see happen. In the process of building that mental image, he often discovers pieces that are needed in the mental model that he hadn't thought about before.

This process allows him to look at things in a three-dimensional fashion. It's a model as opposed to a plan. Architects have plans but they also build models of what they are going to create, because sometimes by turning it around and looking at it from different angles, you see things you don't see when you look at things in a flat representation.

Mental imagery is a technique for problem solving. You can enhance the possibility of building and shaping the future by creating a mental model of what you want to build. In doing so, you are focusing the energy that is necessary to build something at the very beginning of the process. It has been said that the longest journey starts with a single step. When you start building a mental model, that is the single step that starts the journey. The first step is often the toughest, but it's that first step that can move you in the right direction.

In terms of shaping the future, empowering leaders use mental imagery to formulate a vision of the future that they are hoping to bring into reality. They carry the imagery with them and visit it at will. It's like a computer file, there for us to open in its latest iteration having clicked the *save* button. We can continually use it as a reference to compare how things are shaping up compared to what we envisioned. It is both an iterative and a creative process where our mental image helps us further shape reality. In turn, as reality unfolds, it helps us reshape our image. The process is not static. It is dynamic.

This process can also be used with a group. An empowering leader might say, "We are working on problem X. Let's take the next few minutes to sit quietly. I want you to close your eyes and envision a particular solution to problem X or envision a particular aspect of the future that we are talking about creating." The members of the group then share their respective images, critique each other, and use synergy to create a composite image incorporating the best elements of each to come up with a common visualization that taps into their collective inner knowing.

USING VISUALIZATION AS A MENTAL REHEARSAL OF A DESIRED OUTCOME

Visualization is a mental rehearsal of a desired outcome because you are visualizing it before the fact. Otherwise, it would be a memory. It is the prospective playing out of something that you would like to see happen. The first time you do that you're starting to create the picture. If you repeat it, you are starting to create the grooves. You're laying down the tracks. The more you do it, the more power you're putting into it and the more you are shaping your own behavior.

The fact is that repetition, as with any skill, hones that skill. When you practice a tennis stroke, there is a visual as well as a physical component. In your mind's eye you have a visualization of becoming a good tennis player, and you're also using visualization to groove your stroke.

If you're a golfer and you practice your swing by hitting a bucket of balls, you're in essence trying to groove your swing. You're trying to create a behavior, skills, and an approach that will then carry forward the next time you go out and play on a course. The more you do of that, and the more you rehearse it, the more likely you are of seeing the outcomes you want to see.

One of our friend's daughters is an actress. She frequently visualizes the play she is in as part of her rehearsal process. She sees herself playing the role, and then she goes from there. In leadership or in sports, you mentally rehearse the outcome you want to see happen.

The mental rehearsal process is powerful. Its effects can be positive or negative depending upon what we envision. People who worry incessantly and who visualize things going wrong are mentally rehearsing those outcomes. That's why it's important to engage in *fruitful thinkin'* instead of *stinkin' thinkin'*. Leaders who engage in negative mental rehearsals are not grooving their stroke. They're putting it in a rut.

We advocate visualization of desired outcomes, but we need to be aware that the technique is so powerful that we can manifest undesired outcomes if that's where our visualization energy goes. If we find our visualization going to dark places or going to places that are not desirable to us, then we need to interrupt that process and redirect it toward the fruitful version.

USING VISUAL IMAGERY TO
FOSTER DESIRED OUTCOMES

In this section, we are shifting our focus from visualization in the mind to visual imagery in physical reality. We are looking at the power of media and the power of pictures and visual images. Earlier, we wrote about symbols, artifacts, and talisman, some of which exist in the form of visual images. It has been said that a picture is worth a thousand words. As empowering leaders, we can be on the lookout for images that portray what we are trying to create. We often discuss themes in movies that powerfully represent the core values we write about. It could be a photograph, drawing, or a painting that is realistic or abstract. It could be a cartoon or some form multimedia presentation that involves imagery. Such visuals can focus the attention of others in a way that energizes and contributes to the outcomes we are seeking.

All of our senses can lead toward using the power of visual imagery. David has a friend whose son, when in high school, was a soccer player. Before all his soccer games, he would play the music from *Chariots of Fire* because it triggered in his mind the imagery from that movie of running a good race, overcoming obstacles, and winning. For him, it was an energizing activity.

Many athletes use music to workout, train, and prep for a game. The music often triggers a visual image. It's not the music per se; it's the translation of the music into a visual image that creates the power for them, in terms of getting themselves charged up and ready for the game. Visualize the theme from *Rocky,* and visualize Rocky Balboa going up the steps and raising his hands in triumph at the top of the steps of the library. Our colleague Larry used to listen to the theme from *Les Miserable* before a job interview or a public forum dealing with a charged issue. He knew he would be challenged to fight the good fight and he wanted to be at the top of his game.

Movies are replete with visual images that are incredibly powerful magnets for people. We also know that visual imagery can prove to be negative if used in the wrong way. It can fill up the dark spaces. We know that visual images of people killing other people may trigger, in damaged folks, the desire to go out and do likewise. Because visual imagery is so powerful, you have to be careful with it.

We know someone who had the opportunity to talk with director Steven Spielberg about that very issue. Spielberg shared how he had used his movies to try to create a better world by creating stories and images that took people toward their best selves; he opined that many others in his field had different priorities. He very clearly understood the power he had in his hands as a director to create visual images that would move people toward certain behaviors and toward certain ends. Therefore, he felt he had a real responsibility to make sure that what he did was of a nature that allowed people to go toward their higher nature. As empowering leaders, we can draw from an endless array of images to foster positive outcomes and achieve success.

USING VISUALIZATION AS A MEDITATIVE TECHNIQUE

When David wants to put himself into a relaxed state of consciousness, there is a place he goes in his mind that is peaceful and beautiful, and that puts him into a sense of mellow repose. He calls it his "happy place," and he can go there almost at will. If he has to go to the doctor to get a shot or to the dentist to have some work done, he invariably goes to that space to get past the unpleasant experience. In his mind's eye, he puts himself by a stream in Provo Canyon, Utah, listens to the brook and looks at the leaves on the trees and at the flowing water. That's the visual image he uses to put himself into a quieter and less tense and more serene mental state.

That is an example of a powerful technique that empowering leaders, and those they lead, should have in their toolbox. There are times when we need a place like that to retreat to, to recharge. Earlier, we wrote about the power of symbols. Many people have religious symbols that are powerful for them. There are other symbols that have special meaning because they are connected to a loving relationship, or with an achievement, or a sense of purpose.

There is a symbol our colleague Larry knows stands for divine light. He can visualize that symbol in his mind's eye, and it facilitates a quiet and peaceful state of mind. It is the quieting of the mind that fosters a meditative state, which is a particular state of consciousness. There are countless numbers of books that describe different forms of meditation and different techniques for meditating. Many of them use some form of visualization, others use breathing techniques, mantras, chanting, or symbols as methods of entering a meditative state.

There are many purposes for meditating, but at the very least empowering leaders will find such practices to be both relaxing and energizing. Meditative practices can last for a few minutes or a much longer timeframe depending upon your goals. Larry finds the process to be very efficient. By meditating for ten minutes, he feels he gains hours of increased energy.

Using all these techniques will allow you to find the right road for success in your work.

TO BECOME A MORE EMPOWERING LEADER

- Use the power of visualization.
- Use the power of symbols.
- See with your third or inner eye.
- Use mental imagery to solve problems and shape the future.
- Use visualization as a mental rehearsal of desired outcomes.
- Use visual imagery to foster desired outcomes.
- Use visualization as a meditative technique.

Core Value 8

Using Expectation to Achieve Results

EXPECTATION IS AN IMPORTANT
VALUE FOR EMPOWERING LEADERS

We have all seen leaders who are clear about their expectations, and the organization seems to rise or fall to meet them. People adjust their behavior to meet the leader's expectations. It is important for the leader to understand the power of expectations and to understand that her expectations will *set the bar* for the organization.

Expectation sets the stage for people. It presents marching orders for the organization. But it also opens up possibilities for people. An empowering leader should have greater expectations for the organization and its people than the people have for themselves. The leader sets the standard for the organization. High expectations create a high standard, and low expectations inhibit the organization and its people.

Expectations are quantitative because they create the amplitude of the organization. They create the outcomes, rubrics and measures for the organization. They determine how high an organization can soar. But expectations are also qualitative and set the attitude for the organization. Expectations prime the pump. They allow the ideas and work to flow. Everything flows from the leader's expectations. Expectations set the quality for the work.

Another way to look at expectations is that they are the affirmations of the organization in action. They are the affirmations of potential and possibility. When the leader sets a high expectation she is affirming what the person and the organization can become. Expectations are so much more effective than standards. Standards are externally set measures. Expectations, if handled properly, become internalized by people. As they move from the outside to the inside, personal ownership is created.

71

When a leader is content to merely set standards for people, the best that can happen is that adherence and compliance are created. When an expectation is set and internalized, you can never tell the heights that might be achieved because it is something they own. They may even decide the leader isn't really expecting enough and go well beyond the initial expectation. This creates dynamism in the organization.

The power of expectation is directly proportional to its authenticity. When expectation is contrived it doesn't have the same power as it does when it comes from an authentic sense of what is possible. If you are a leader who really believes that people are capable and willing to do their best and that they are capable and willing to be creative and to take the initiative, that will become the reality of the organization because the leader is behaving with authentic expectations. People will choose to align themselves with that view.

Most people want to meet or exceed your expectation. It pulls the best out of them. There is really nothing more powerful than believing in someone else. The strongest words a leader can utter are, "I believe in you." This offers the ultimate trust in another and it is incredibly powerful.

Leadership is ultimately about the interactions that the leader has with the individuals in the organization. Leaders are role models, and leaders must first have high expectations for themselves. People will see that and respond accordingly.

EXPECTATION HELPS TO SHAPE REALITY

Thoughts create reality. In essence, you can create a reality by what and how you think. Proverbs reminds us that "as a man thinketh, so he is." The act of thought creates reality. When a leader sets expectations he is creating the reality for the organization. It is important for a leader to treat people not as they are but as they might become. People will usually rise to that higher expectation.

Occasionally, people will disappoint you, but it has been our experience that more often than not, people will rise to the challenge. Setting high expectations is also setting a higher level of reality. Expectations set the goals, but they also create the game plan, and, most important, the energy to make it so.

There are different ways to articulate the expectations for the organization. They can be spoken, written, or even expressed in symbols or mottos. This allows them to become mental constructs of what is desired and what can be. This presents a schema for the organization, which allows everyone to draw upon their creativity and their gifts to align with those expectations.

This is a continual shaping process. The expectations have to be continually projected outward to the organization. This also allows the leader and the organization to monitor how they are progressing toward the expectations. This also allows for adjustment and refinement to occur while the organization moves toward the initial expectation.

Expectations are as much about the process as they are about the end product. You are not just defining the end of the journey but also the quality of the journey. That is really an act of leadership because ultimately leadership isn't merely setting the goals; it is also escorting people to the goals.

It is incumbent upon leaders to have positive expectations. If the leader has a negative expectation for those in the organization, it will be impossible to achieve positive outcomes in the organization's goals. Whatever the leader feels about her expectation for others will become a self-fulfilling prophecy for the organization. Leaders must paint pictures of possibility for those in the organization so that it can move in the desired direction.

When a leader is cynical and lacks that sense of positive possibility, she limits what the organization can achieve. She creates a small box of possibilities. When a leader lacks trust in those with whom they work, she cannot create more than a constricted vision for the organization. We all have seen the signs that say, "The beatings will continue until morale improves," and recognize the humor in it. However, it is amazing how many leaders actually act as though they want to follow that dictum.

People rise or fall to the level of the expectations set for them. When a leader is controlling or cynical, they cannot set high expectations. To do so is dishonest. If you can't believe in others, you cannot expect much from them. Leaders either turn lights on or turn lights off. They either illuminate the room for others so they can see their possibilities or they create an atmosphere of darkness, which means the organization will stumble around and bump into the furniture and itself.

HIGH EXPECTATIONS SHOULD START WITH OURSELVES

It is silly to set high expectations for others and not have them for yourself. You can't expect others to sacrifice if you will not do so yourself. What we *do* as a leader speaks much more loudly than what we *say*. How you act as a leader will determine your effectiveness. There has to be an alignment between what you say your expectations are and what your behaviors are. Leaders, through their actions, set the tone for their expectations for the organization.

It is important to understand that self-confident behavior can sometimes be perceived as arrogance. It is important that the leader not set herself apart from those who work with her. An empowering leader understands they need other people. By letting others know that they are needed and believed in, the leader creates energy in the organization for getting things done. The teaching of Taoism reminds us that it is best that when the work is done, the people say, "We did it ourselves." Leaders must have a belief in self but that should not trump their belief in others.

Leaders must remember that anything taken to an extreme becomes perverted. Self-confidence slides into arrogance. High expectations can quickly become coercion. Too much reliance on others can become abrogation of responsibility. As high expectations are set for self and others, it is critical that a sense of balance is maintained. Leaders must guard against becoming coercive and manipulative as they move the organization toward high expectations.

This leads to the necessity of the leader remembering what their purpose is. When one has a higher purpose, he or she will be much less likely to abuse others around them. Your purpose helps set the conditions for your behavior. If your purpose is "other directed," then your leadership style and your own behavior will be shaped in that direction. When you have a more self-centered purpose, your behavior will be less open and positive and ultimately less empowering.

When we have high expectations we must remember there are several elements involved. One is in terms of our own performance, our own work ethic, and our own commitment to the expectations of the organization. But there is also the element of our belief in others and the expectations we have for them. A leader needs three lenses operating simultaneously; one for him- or herself, one for the other people in the organization, and one for the corporate good of the organization and its mission.

An empowering leader has two ways of seeing others. One sight is like x-ray vision, where the leader looks inside himself and inside those who work with him and sees what is there and what the possibilities are for that person. Most of us have had other people see potential in us that we didn't see for ourselves. That came from their x-ray vision, which tends to raise the bar and open new vistas of opportunity and potential in us and in others.

The other vision is seeing how that potential we see in others and ourselves affects the organization. You don't merely see the potential; you also have a vision of that potential fulfilled. You see how that internal power can be manifested. This allows the leader to maintain a vision for those around them and how they might impact the organization.

PEOPLE WILL STRIVE TO JUSTIFY OUR FAITH IN THEM

While it would be magic if everyone justified our faith in them, it is clear that not everyone is willing to accept that justification. However, most people want to rise to others' expectations. All humans have their moments of insecurity and feeling of inadequacy. But beyond that we must help them not fear their power.

As the poet Marianne Williamson pointed out, "Our deepest fear is not that we are inadequate. Our deepest fear is that we are powerful beyond measure. It is our light, not our darkness that we fear the most." The leader's role is to help people not fear their inadequacies or their strengths.

Most people *want* to be empowered, but they must conquer their fears and their moments of doubt. The authors feel that we are all given a spark of light that makes great things possible in us. We also understand that the world can conspire against us and it is sometimes hard to keep that spark lit. It beats us down and makes us question our potential. It is incumbent on all of us, particularly empowering leaders, to rekindle and nurture that spark of light.

We do this by having a belief and faith in others. We can show that faith in a thousand ways. We can tell them how much we believe in them. We can give them a job to do and trust their actions. We can smile or nod at them or even pat them on the back. This belief can be a powerful motivating force in their lives. External support can light the fire within them.

When it comes down to it, we have met few people who set out to be failures or who want to do a poor job. Sometimes their lack of knowledge or skill inhibits them, and sometimes it is their lack of belief in themselves. We can help them gain the knowledge and skills to do the job. We can also affirm them in ways that strengthen their self-belief.

When your belief in another person is genuine, they know it. And this creates a positive and even synergistic loop in them where success builds upon success. When they know your faith is genuine, they work to justify that faith. Then, when you affirm their progress, they try even harder. As you reinforce your belief in them, they move further in the desired direction. It becomes a dance of possibility becoming reality.

POSITIVE EXPECTATIONS
FOSTER POSITIVE OUTCOMES

As leaders, we always have a choice of which side of the mountain we want to roll the rock down. When you choose the right side of the mountain, it makes it very difficult for the rock to change course. We create a force where gravity takes control and it speeds up the rolling rock and builds on its momentum. Once you set loose a positive expectation, it is very difficult for negative outcomes to ensue.

Sometimes the rock can get caught up partway down the mountain, but you are still better off than if you had rolled it down the negative side of the mountain. Progress has been made. Setting positive expectations creates positive outcomes.

External forces can affect the degree of success and the outcome may not be completely fulfilled, but you are still better off than you would have been if you had not had those positive expectations. The key is to take action. Setting a positive expectation is the first action. That action creates energy that leads toward the place you want to go. The degree to which you pursue it, the enthusiasm you have for it, and the energy you put into it will all affect the final outcome and your final success. But there is no question that when you set positive expectations you begin moving things down the positive side of the mountain.

Most leaders will tell you they want positive outcomes. We are living in a time where outcomes and performance and results are critical aspects of leadership. So the question becomes how you produce them. You do that by setting expectations, monitoring their progress, reshaping them and making certain that energy is invested in them. When you see a positive outcome, you can feel certain it grew from a positive set of expectations.

WE ARE THE MIRRORS THROUGH
WHICH OTHERS SEE THEMSELVES

Our self-image impacts how we respond to the world. Each of us has a sense of who we are, what our capabilities are, what gifts we possess, what our weaknesses are and what we are about. How do we know this? We learn them by looking at others and by receiving feedback from others. We have images of ourselves, but are they accurate? To better understand ourselves, we use others as a mirror that reflects images back to us. This is one important way expectations get set.

The mirror must have a focus to it. There is a mirror, which is often used by women who are putting on their makeup or men who are trying to shave, that magnifies and focuses on a small area. This is the kind of feedback mirror that best helps us help others understand and see their best selves. It is important that attention is drawn to the qualities that need to be focused upon.

Beyond the focused mirror, we need to act as an x-ray machine that looks inside the other person and allows us to show them things about themselves they may never have noticed before. We heard of one leader who had struggled in school. When he got to high school, he had a teacher who asked him which college he was planning to attend. It hadn't occurred to him that he was capable of even going to college, but she saw something he didn't see and she helped him focus on that possibility.

This behavior is repeated over and over as we find mentors or act as mentors to others. Mentors are really those focused mirrors/x-rays that we need to find our potential and nurture it. One of the most powerful questions we can ask someone else is "Have you ever thought about doing this or trying that?" All of us have had that question posed to us (or should have), and most of the time we haven't actually thought about it. But those questions plant seeds of possibility that can grow in a brighter future.

We all remember the movie *Snow White and the Seven Dwarfs* and the question of "mirror, mirror on the wall, who's the fairest of them all?" That mirror could see the truth, which didn't make the wicked stepmother very happy. Good mirrors reflect, focus, and highlight what *is*. A great mirror also highlights what *might be.*

That mirror of expectation has the power to unleash human potential and that is the real essence of empowering leadership. It also marks the difference between being a manager who sees things as they are and empowering leaders who see what might be.

OTHERS ARE THE MIRRORS
THROUGH WHICH WE SEE OURSELVES

While the feedback from others is critical to our seeing ourselves, it is also important that we fact check the feedback. Sometimes you might find that the feedback is distorted, but it is always good to stay open to what you are hearing. When the feedback seems really off, you might consider that the person is describing himself more than he is describing you.

To be honest, we probably do that to others even with the best of intentions. It is important that the mirror we are holding up reflects accurately and that we look for the accuracy in the mirror others are holding up for us. If we realize we are reflecting ourselves onto others, it does give us some real truth about ourselves.

The key to providing a mirror or judging a mirror is to have a benevolent attitude. When we are serving others, we hold up a benevolent mirror. It comes from a positive place and the criticism or insights are positive. On the other side, judgment of others (or a harsh judgment of ourselves) is not useful.

Sometimes it is better to act more as a window so that the other person can see clearly through it to make their own decisions rather than dealing with your judgment. That way they can see the real person and penetrate to a deeper level of understanding.

Another way to see how others provide a mirror for us is to envision a room full of mirrors. Each reflects a part of who we are. It is up to us to decide what the three-dimensional person is. Leaders need to do reality checks to see how they look to others. Sometimes it may feel accurate, and sometimes it may feel inaccurate.

If you decide it is inaccurate you might want to ask yourself why they have a picture of you that does not comport with your own assessment.

Empowering leaders have to be open to seeing themselves as others see them, even if that creates cognitive dissonance. Then the job becomes how to reduce that dissonance. It is also important that we understand that our feedback might be creating dissonance in others. This would allow a united front on pursuing the expectations we have for others and the organization.

EMPOWERING LEADERS UNDERSTAND

- Expectation is an important value for empowering leaders.
- Expectation helps shape reality.
- High expectations must start with themselves.
- People will strive to justify our faith in them.
- Positive expectations foster positive outcomes.
- We are mirrors through which others see themselves.
- Others are mirrors through which we see ourselves.

Intuition—Discovering Our Hidden Knowledge

INTUITION IS AN IMPORTANT RESOURCE FOR EMPOWERING LEADERS

Accepting intuition as a part of your life is taking a leap into the unknown. To truly be an empowering leader, you have to be prepared to lead into the void between what you know and what you feel. You have to go beyond what is logical and rational and acknowledge there is more than we can know with our conscious mind.

When you accept that intuition is real, you have moved from the realm of the rational toward a state of enlightened awareness. To be fully empowered and empowering, you have to accept that there is a space you cannot fully explain that allows you to make decisions and to take actions that go beyond your perceived limitations. It is an act of faith—a belief in the unseen. Yet, current literature on leadership is fraught with implications of intuition. All great leaders act from knowing things, but they also act from feeling them. Intuition doesn't live in your head—it resides in your gut.

The role of leadership is so involved and so complex there are times when you have to act without having all the information you need. At those moments, you have to act on instinct and use your intuition, which, in part, is the accumulated wisdom you have attained from a lifetime of living.

If you lead a small organization you can rely on having a lot of information available to make a decision. As the organization grows or if you move to a larger organization, you will have the same amount of relative information but the percentage of what you know will be much smaller. More will be unknown. You still have to decide, but with less information. Intuition becomes invaluable.

This is also true as change and the influx of information comes to us at lightning speed. Leaders in today's world are inundated with challenges and bits and bytes of information and are required to act with great speed. How can this be done? It must involve the use of our inner wisdom. We have to trust the deeper parts of ourselves to access the proper course of action.

The good news is that a willingness to use your intuition also offers greater vistas of opportunity to make decisions and go in directions that might not have been considered before. There is a broader spectrum of options available.

The first requirement for accessing your intuition is to remain open. You have to be open to the reality of intuition and also be open to the information and wisdom that is flowing through you. Allied with your openness is trust. You have to be able to trust yourself and your instincts. You have to be open to your feelings and your gut.

We have all experienced intuition whether or not we label it as such. We have all had the experience of meeting someone and knowing something about them without knowing why. We know more than we have any right to know based upon the evidence we have. Sometimes we have a sense about an event that turns out to be very accurate. How did we know? Intuition.

Another way to understand intuition is to understand how our brain works. We each have two sides to the brain. The left side gives us the capacity to think in a logical, orderly fashion. The right side operates more holistically. It gathers a lot of information from many different sources and allows us to respond creatively. You can look at intuition as another way of accessing your right brain. You are merely assessing the thought processes there and trusting them. You also have to be open to the signals your unconscious brain is sending.

INTUITION IS ANOTHER WAY OF KNOWING

For some of us, intuition makes us even surer of what we know. If we trust our intuition, it reinforces the more rational parts of our understanding. An intuitive leader feels guided by his intuition. Using the left, more rational side of your brain forces you to look at all the facts and information. But what happens when you don't have all the facts and you must still decide? Intuition allows you to see the path that you must follow. This gives a sense of real certainty to a leader.

On the other hand it is very difficult to explain your thinking to someone else. They will want to know *how* you know, and you, of course, can't really explain *how* you know. This can make them a bit uncertain. This can also create conflict between the leader and the led, but you have to remain certain in your knowing and stick with it.

President George W. Bush once observed that he liked being president because he didn't have to explain himself. He felt he knew what he knew. One might argue whether all of his decisions were the right ones, but he was courageous enough to follow his instincts. It is clear that intuition isn't always going to be correct. You might be ignoring information that would lead to a different conclusion or you might have read your gut incorrectly and the wrong outcome ensues, but that doesn't invalidate the value of intuition. It serves as a caution to you. It is a yellow light, not a red or green one.

Empowering leaders have to make certain that they have intellectual capital and lots of information and facts so they can use the left side of their brain. But they must also remain open to the wisdom that the right side of the brain offers them. Using your intuition allows you to combine what you know in your mind and what you feel in your heart. When those are aligned, the right course is clear.

Intuition allows the right answer to appear, sometimes without the need to walk through all the intervening steps. Intuition allows you to *cut to the chase*. This can cause problems in some areas. Math teachers want you to show your work, and if you are getting the answers intuitively they don't really understand that. This is the reason one of us majored in English in college rather than math!

EMPOWERING LEADERS SHOULD STRIVE TO TRUST THEIR INTUITION AND FEELINGS

Given the complexity, ambiguity, and myriad challenges facing leaders today, we need all the help we can get. Intuition is the "secret sauce" of effective, empowering leaders. But you have to use it. Intuition is like a special muscle but it must be used to be strong. If you have intuitive insights and you fail to act on them, and this happens repeatedly, the intuiting will weaken and you will doubt its power. If you pay attention to your intuition and use it, it comes more easily to you.

Intuition is that small inner voice that tells you what you should do. When you ignore that voice, it weakens and eventually fails to be available to you. You have to be open to hearing that voice and acting upon it. Intuition is something that builds upon itself. The more it is used, the more frequently it appears.

You could argue that intuition hits us viscerally. It is often a feeling more than a complete thought. Sometimes you get the feeling about someone or something that it is just "off." It doesn't feel right. Other times you get a feeling that is so right, you just know it is the thing to do or the person that you should listen to.

One of the interesting things about intuition is that you can't force it to happen. You can't pursue it. It is just there. In Eastern philosophy there is a saying that when the student is ready, the teacher appears. Intuition acts very much the same way. When you are open to it, it happens.

The following story illustrates this point. There once was a river cruise on the Amazon River. One of the many interesting attractions of the Amazon is that it is the only place in the world that has fresh water dolphins—and they are pink! Of course everyone wanted to see the pink dolphins. One day the guides took all the travelers out to an area known for the dolphins so they could see them. After several hours of vigorous searching, the mission was a failure. No pink dolphins. The boat had to leave that area of the river and move on downstream. Everyone was disappointed.

The next morning the boat was moored and the passengers could hear funny noises outside. When they went out they found the boat surrounded by pink dolphins. They had come to the voyagers. Sometimes the things we pursue the hardest will prove elusive, but if you can relax and stay open and ready, they may come to you as the pink dolphins did.

IT IS HELPFUL FOR EMPOWERING LEADERS TO SEE INTUITION AS A SIXTH SENSE

We are all familiar with our five senses. But what if there is a sixth sense? What if there is something beyond what we can hear, see, feel, touch, or smell with our physical senses? For centuries, man thought that the only things that existed were what could be witnessed with their five senses. Yet technology has shown that isn't true. We have equipment that shows there is a light spectrum far beyond the power of our eyes to see. We have machines that can sense sounds far beyond the capacity of our ears to hear. So too is it with intuition. Intuition allows us to see and hear what we cannot witness with our physical senses.

Trying to explain intuition is like trying to explain eyesight. You can talk about the lens of your eye, the optic nerve that carries the image to your brain and all the millions of small parts that go into letting you see, but despite the scientific explanation, seeing a field of flowers or a sunset is just as magical as having a sense of intuition about people or plans. Is the process of seeing a field of flowers and feeling its beauty really that much different than gaining an insight?

From research we know that the right side of our brain processes faster than the left side of the brain. One is analog, and the other is digital. Our right brain does the processing that allows what is in our subconscious to become conscious. This is the process of intuition. So it is really like having another sense. The process involves taking information that is outside ourselves and gathering and sorting it unconsciously and then drawing upon information we have already stored in our mind and putting it all together.

Malcolm Gladwell, in his book *Blink*, describes the process in action. He says true experts can look at a piece of art that others have studied intensely and determined to be original and know that it is a fake in the split second it takes to look at it. They just "know" it is a forgery without doing all the tests and research. Intuition operates with the blink of an eye. Intuition allows you to know more than you know.

Intuition is also making yourself available to the knowledge that exists outside you. We are all familiar with the question that asks, "If a tree falls in the forest and there is no one there to hear it, does it make a sound?" The answer is yes and no. It does create sound waves that move out from its falling. If there were someone near, they would hear it. However, the issue is that for something to be deemed real, it has to be received and processed. The universe is sending us signals and information all the time. If we are open to receiving them, they become part of our knowing.

You might think of your intuition as a tuning fork. The more you use it, the more effective it is as a tool. When you are attuned, the world opens to you.

If you talked to someone who uses their intuition repeatedly, they will tell you that the only times it has failed them is when they ignored it. You might think of intuition as a truth serum that points the way for you to do the right thing.

The problem is that sometimes what our intuition is telling us is not what we want to hear. Maybe it's not what we want to see happen or it may be disconcerting. An intuitive leader heard a message on his home answering machine intended for his wife. It was from his wife's new student teacher. He knew from hearing the message the student teacher was going to be difficult to work with and probably would not succeed. He couldn't really say how, but he knew. He didn't say anything to his wife because he didn't want to create a self-fulfilling prophecy. Unfortunately, the student teacher did turn out to be very difficult to work with and was a problem for his wife. In hindsight, not sharing the intuition may have been an error because she didn't know what she was getting into.

Intuition is really about connecting the dots. The universe gives us the dots and we need to connect them. In the case of the overheard message, the husband picked up certain rational pieces of information, but there were feelings generated that connected the dots and told the husband that his wife was in for trouble with that person. The problem is some of the dots were easy to prove; others were feelings. He didn't want to act on the feelings and be unfair to the new colleague. In hindsight, he should have acted on his intuition.

HOW EMPOWERING LEADERS CAN BECOME MORE INTUITIVE

One of the things a leader can do is to conduct a reality check on her intuition. She should track over time how accurate and effective her intuition is. It is one thing to rely on your intuition but quite another to discover that it is ineffective. Intuition should be highly accurate or you are just acting under impulse but not connected to your inner wisdom.

Intuition is essentially an internal process that must be verified externally. On one hand, if information comes from outside, it must be checked internally. On the other hand, if you operate solely on internal bias, processes, and thoughts, your reactions may come off as illogical, incomplete, or inappropriate with a flawed outcome. To become effective, you must marry the external factors with your internal instincts. A total reliance on external factors ignores your inner wisdom, and a total reliance on internal instincts makes you impulsive and wrong. Intuition is powerful, but it must always be checked against reality.

It is easier for some people to use their intuition than it is for others. Again, the more one becomes comfortable with their intuition and the more they use it, the better they become at making it work for them. As we have already observed, trust becomes an essential element in intuition, but it is not enough to merely trust the process; you must become comfortable trusting trust itself. If you are not a person who is comfortable with trust as a core value, then it will be very difficult to access your intuition.

If you cannot trust, you will create blocks to accepting your inner wisdom. You won't trust it. That also means you don't really trust yourself. So, before you can really use your intuition, you have to work on trusting others and yourself.

You have to be open and trusting and then you can gain the flow that comes from putting the outside and the inside together. You want to make certain that you do not constrict the channels that are at work. You want to open the channels so that you can be in a state of flow. This gives you access to all the dots and makes it easier to connect them. The more dots you have, the clearer the picture becomes.

INTUITION IS ONE OF THE WAYS IN WHICH WE
RECEIVE COMMUNICATION FROM OUR HIGHER SELF

It is possible to use your intuition without a belief in your higher self, but the reality is that we all have a higher self. You don't have to have a spiritual side to recognize that there is a part of you that is purer and has a better impulse than the rest of you. Lincoln called it "our better angels." There is a part of us that wants what is best for us and it reminds us of that.

Another way to look at your higher self is to imagine that there is a drone flying overhead that sees more than you can see at ground level. It is your own personal camera that gives you the lay of the land in a way you can't see. Our higher self is that part of us that is above the rest of us. It has a better angle and perspective. When you get connected to that, you have a better picture of things.

In the Civil War, they sent people up in balloons so they could see the battlefield and could come back and tell the generals what was happening. Today, we use drones, reconnaissance planes, and satellites. It is clear that the higher up you are, the more complete the picture you have. You can look over the horizon and see what is coming. The greater perspective you have the better prepared you are to face the unknown.

What we experience as intuition can come from many different sources. One is our subconscious mind. We know that the subconscious mind is always working. It is processing what our conscious mind is gathering. We also believe there is a higher self, or soul, working on our behalf. It also informs and guides us. If you are spiritual, you also believe that your higher self is connected to an infinite intelligence, which may be called source, God, the divine, a force greater than man—and countless other names—that is also available for assistance.

We believe that there are times when that higher force speaks to us through our intuition. It may be difficult to determine whether the source is divine, our higher self, or merely our unconscious that gives us insight through our intuition. Regardless of its origin, it is a source of wisdom that is real and available to you.

For thousands of years, theologians have discussed the way the divine may speak to us. In the Judeo-Christian tradition, God spoke in very direct ways. He delivered his laws to Moses on stone tablets, and he spoke to Saul as a burning bush on the road to Damascus. Most of us haven't had that dramatic interaction, but that doesn't necessarily mean that the divine doesn't speak to us. One of the ways this happens is through our higher selves.

WAYS IN WHICH EMPOWERING LEADERS
CAN ASSESS HOW INTUITIVE THEY ARE

There are actually personality assessments that can help leaders understand their own leadership style and therefore understand their own abilities in using intuition. For example, the Meyers-Briggs Personality Inventory tells you where you stand on the intuitive-sensing front. The instrument has a scale that shows a continuum of various traits. Some people fall on the far end of the intuition continuum. Others are more adept at using their five senses. Someone in the middle of the continuum gives equal weight to intuiting and sensing. This offers self-knowledge for you, the leader, in understanding where you might be on the continuum of using your intuition.

A very right-brained leader uses holistic assessment to determine what is true. He self-checks his own intuition by listening to the words he uses. If he finds himself saying, "I think" a lot instead of "I feel," he knows he is probably not tapping into his own intuition as much as he should because his thinking brain has not always been as accurate as his use of feelings. In the Meyers-Briggs Personality Inventory, he is an intuitive-feeling type.

A left-brain dominant leader uses facts and logic to a great extent in his decision making. He checks on his intuition by seeing how fast he makes a decision. If he is making lightning-quick decisions, he knows he is using his intuition. The speed of the decision tells him whether he is merely using his five senses or has tapped into his intuitive sixth sense. In the Meyers-Briggs Personality Inventory, he is an intuitive-thinking type.

Another way to assess how intuitive you are is to monitor how you communicate with others. If you are highly intuitive and the person you are dealing with is also highly intuitive, your communications will also be a form of shorthand. You will not need to explain things. The other person will just "get it." You have a shortcut to each other's subconscious. You connect with each other without knowing how. With others, it doesn't seem to matter how much you talk. You still can't connect.

When one person is intuitive and the other is more reliant on their five senses, the communications can sometimes be more difficult. If you are an intuitive leader, you will need to use more traditional forms of communication to reach those in the organization who are sense based.

The goal for an empowering leader is to create opportunities for unconscious knowing to emerge. When people are engaged in dialogue in a relaxed state, this can occur. Facilitating such interactions can open the spigot in your organization and new ideas will flow and dynamism will pour forth. Those involved will be able to tap into their inner knowledge and the organization will benefit.

EMPOWERING LEADERS CAN ACCESS THEIR HIDDEN KNOWLEDGE BY

- Understanding that intuition is an important resource.
- Knowing what distinguishes intuition from other ways of knowing.

- Understanding that intuition is another way of knowing.
- Striving to trust their intuition and feelings.
- Understanding it is helpful to see intuition as a sixth sense.
- Knowing they can become more intuitive.
- Believing that intuition is one of the ways we receive communications from our higher self.
- Knowing there are ways of assessing how intuitive they are.

Core Value 10

Using Awareness to Expand Our Perspective

We live in an age of information overload. As a leader, what must you be aware of as you lead? What requires your attention and when? What information do you need? What information must you pay attention to, and what can you ignore, and for how long? We not only have to be aware of what's happening in our organization and what external changes may affect it, but we also have to be aware of ourselves and what changes may affect us and our well being.

Like an artist, we have to be able to view things from multiple perspectives, and like a photographer, we need to be able to adjust our field of vision to zoom in and zoom out at will. We not only need to see clearly, but also we have to understand how what we see affects us and our organization.

AWARENESS IS AN IMPORTANT CORE VALUE FOR EMPOWERING LEADERS

At a very basic level, awareness is about paying attention. It's about being open to what's already there. This was driven home to one of our colleagues when he was diagnosed with glaucoma. The colors and scenes and images had always been there, but he had just breezed past them, too busy to pay attention or be open to them. When faced with the threat of losing his vision, he said to himself, "You can't take *seeing* for granted," and suddenly the world opened up. For the first time in his life, he became acutely aware of the vibrancy in the visible world around him. The colors became more vivid, and the scenes became more apparent in his awareness. Now, he would stop and actually look at things. Once his awareness opened, he opened up to a much richer environment.

There are different lenses through which we, as empowering leaders, can perceive reality. We can see things politically, financially, socially, organizationally, and legally from the perspective of the client, the staff, the board, the public, and so forth. The greater variety of lenses that leaders have at their disposal, the more effective and successful they will be. One element of awareness has to do with the viewing instrument, namely, which lens or lenses are we looking *through.*

But another aspect of awareness has to do with what we're looking *at.* Empowering leaders need the ability to not only select the right lens through which to see things and the right focal length in terms of a wide view or focused view, but also be aware as to where to look, and where to focus their attention.

Our environment has become increasingly overwhelming in terms of the visual imagery that surrounds us, the sounds that surround us, and the speed at which things are moving. Our success as empowering leaders depends on our ability to be discerning as to what in our environment we really should pay attention to. We need the ability to be aware of what is most important in the vast panoply of stimuli around us. You have to take a wide-angle view of things and then focus your awareness on those things that require the most attention or would yield the greatest positive outcome.

IT IS IMPORTANT FOR EMPOWERING LEADERS TO BE SELF-AWARE

Self-awareness as it relates to leadership is about alignment and attunement: alignment of your thoughts and deeds, and attunement to your environment. If you're not sufficiently self-aware, your words and deeds may be in conflict with each other. You may appear to lack integrity. Without a good sense of self-awareness, it's fairly easy to lose your sense of integrity because you're not checking yourself in the mirror to see what is really there and to see what others see.

One of the lenses of awareness is a lens for self-awareness. You can think of yourself as putting this lens on to open things up for you to look at. You can look at your own motivation. You can self-check what's motivating you to do what you are doing in any given situation and to decide whether that motivation is appropriate. You can self-check your effect on other people as they respond to your actions. Looking at the effects of what you do is an aspect of self-awareness. That requires some degree of self-reflection. You need to have self-awareness of your feelings and your moods and how your moods affect other people.

We know someone who remembers a time when he was in a rotten mood and everyone around him was looking at themselves to figure out what they were doing wrong. He had enough self-awareness to realize that they were blaming themselves for whatever was happening. He said, "You've got to forgive me. I just happen to be in a really bad mood. You're not doing anything wrong, and I hope you can bear with me until this passes."

Empowering leaders have sufficient self-awareness not to blame other people for things they themselves do or say. The flip side of that is recrimination. The power of self-awareness has to do with seeing ourselves as we are and seeing ourselves as we ought to be and being able to do both of those things without any sense of self-recrimination. You need to be objective about yourself and what you see when you look at yourself. And you need to be objective about the people around you and what you see in them, both positive and negative. You need to be able to help guide them without blaming them for being wrong or being inadequate.

In one of the Harry Potter movies, Professor Dumbledore tells Harry, "Our destiny is not shaped by our talents but by the choices we make." What we are suggesting is that empowering leaders make a choice to be aware, to be self-aware, to be open to the world around us, and to understand that we are responsible for the choices we make. We need not beat ourselves up about our lack of talents or failures. Instead, we should use self-reflection and self-awareness as a way to improve ourselves and those who we lead.

LENSES OF AWARENESS EMPOWERING LEADERS WILL FIND USEFUL

Lenses of awareness are the way we see things. They affect what we see and how we frame what we see.

The Spiritual Lens

Empowering leaders make the world better in ways large and small for themselves, those with whom they work, and their organizations. Leaders who do that see the world through a spiritual lens, although they may not think of it in those terms. We believe that all of us are spiritual beings living in a sacred world. By spiritual we mean that we are connected to one another, to the natural world, and to a force greater than ourselves. Learning to look at mundane aspects of the world through this lens can be useful to leaders because it may provide a broader view of the nature of their work.

The Lens of Light

We live in a polarized world, a world of light and darkness. We think of empowering leaders as warriors of the light. This lens uses metaphors of light: being a visionary, lighting a candle in the darkness, creating a brighter future, shedding light on an issue, seeing the light at the end of the tunnel, being a beacon of light, and so forth. This lens is empowering for the leader and her team.

The Energy Lens

We are *energy beings*. Every living cell in our body is constantly in motion. We each have a personal energy field akin to the field surrounding a magnet. It is useful for empowering leaders to view themselves, other people, systems, their organization, and the environment itself as interconnected energy fields. Understand how to look at things from the point of view of energy in terms of those things that increase energy, those things that decrease it, and those things that replenish it. This is useful to empowering leaders.

The Holistic Lens

Empowering leaders look at things from a holistic perspective. They are able to look at anything and understand that it is always part of something larger. By looking at things from the lens of a holistic perspective, they can see how the elements of a system have an impact on each other and on the whole.

The Lens of Interconnectedness

Empowering leaders have a lens of awareness that allows them to see themselves and others from the perspective of mind, body, and spirit (energy). They understand the interconnectedness of those three aspects of who we are and the need for balance within and among those aspects of our humanity.

The $E=mc^2$ Lens

Empowering leaders have a lens of awareness that allows them to see what is required to create a critical mass, which can shift energy to create outcomes under various circumstances.

They know how to marshal resources and sequence events to create a tipping point for needed organizational change and growth.

The Lens of the Natural World

Empowering leaders not only know that we are connected to the natural world, but they also look to the natural world for lessons that can be applied to their organizations such as the advantages of diversity, how ecosystems thrive or become depleted, balance, and interdependence.

EXPANDING OUR REPERTOIRE OF LENSES OF AWARENESS

As an empowering leader, you can expand your repertoire of lenses of awareness by being open to doing so. You can select one or more of the lenses described in the previous section and start incorporating them into your behaviors. There are things we do today as a leader that we didn't do ten or even twenty years ago because, along the way, we picked techniques or ideas up from someone else. We became aware of ways of being, seeing, or acting that were different than the way we were before; ways that are more effective than what we had been doing.

What happens with leaders is that we fall into patterns of behavior. Often, we don't take the time to ask ourselves, "What are we doing?" "Is this the best course of action?" As an empowering leader, you can promote *reflective practice*, creating situations where you are forced to reflect upon what you are doing. In reflecting upon what you are doing, you are able to see if you are on track or where you might be off track. While being reflective, you can *put on* those other lenses of awareness you may not be capitalizing on yet.

Once you are looking not only *for* lenses of awareness but also *through* lenses of awareness, you become more aware of the different ways you can look at things, as well as the option you have to focus on the foreground or background in any situation. In terms of the lenses themselves, in any given circumstance, you can ask yourself, "Are there any spiritual lessons being presented here? Are there any life lessons that are occurring for me or for the organization? Is there an opportunity here to express gratitude? Are there any lessons in nature that can guide me in terms of what is happening?"

Or, just look at people's reactions and ask yourself, "What is happening with the energy flow? Is there anything I can do to alter the energy flow that would be expansive?" By asking yourself these types of questions you can bring into focus some other aspect of what is going on around you and then take action that will move things in a positive direction.

Having different lenses of awareness is like going to the eye doctor, where they flip the lenses and ask, "Is this better or is that better? Does this make it clearer? Does this make it less clear? At a certain point you get clarity.

Unfortunately, it's not a state that you achieve and maintain. What's clear today is foggy tomorrow. The fog rolls back in and you're right back trying to cut through it again. You continually have to readjust, stop, and try on these different lenses so that you can see where you are. We need to adjust to get back on a track or we end up going down the wrong path, stumbling into holes because we aren't sufficiently aware of the world around us, or the complexity of situations we're facing.

TRYING TO SEE FROM MULTIPLE VANTAGE POINTS

If you only look through your own vantage point, you never see the world through anyone else's perspective. You can't be an empowering leader without having a certain level of empathy and being able, as President Clinton used to say, " *to feel their pain.*" You've got to be able to, in a genuine way, feel what the other person is feeling. The ability to see the world through someone else's eyes is very important when you're in a leadership position.

The more vantage points that we use, the more likely it is that we are seeing the whole. Multiple vantage points allow us to get a more holistic view of whatever it is we're looking at. The more we are aware of the different perspectives, or points of view, for any issue we are considering, the more we can factor those into our decision-making processes. It's good for us, as leaders, to be able to step back, and even step around to look at things in different ways. It's also good to utilize the people who are in our sphere to find out what the issue looks like to them, because it may look very different to them than it looks to us.

International travel broadens your perspective. Someone we know entered a classroom in Australia and noticed a world map hanging on the wall. Australia was in the center of the map! He thought, "What the heck is that about?" He realized that, in the United States, we're in the center of the map, but in Australia, it is Australia that is in the center of the maps. And it was interesting, because when he was in Southeast Asia, it was the center of the world map. North America is off to the side. Every nation has its own perspective. None of them are wrong, but they are incomplete. So what you need are multiple perspectives to come up with a more complete picture.

This is true at the micro level as well as a macro level. We have a friend who has an outdoor spa. The spa has five places to sit and two places to recline. Each seat gives you a different view of the surrounding grounds. From some seats you can see 40 yards to the tree line, from others you can see 100 yards to 200 yards. From some seats you can see a water feature, from others you can just hear the flow of the water. From the recliner you can see the tops of 75-foot trees and the sky overhead. Each seat has a unique perspective as well as a unique arrangement of the water and air jets. If six people were in the spa each would be seeing something and feeling something different. Only by changing seats or exchanging information can the whole be perceived and understood. A single vantage point is just too limiting.

EXPANDING OUR AWARENESS AND FIELD OF VISION

Expanding our awareness has to do with our own growth, and our own capacity to be life-long learners. Awareness is related to what it is we know, and what it is we have been taught to see and appreciate. If we take a course in modern art, we gain an awareness of the subtleties of modern art that we wouldn't have if we didn't have that new knowledge. If we go into the woods with a naturalist, and the naturalist points out which things can be eaten to survive and which things are poisonous, and how things are related in an ecosystem, then when we come back, we see that environment in a different way because we know more.

So one way of expanding our awareness is to continually work at expanding the knowledge that we have in our field, and the knowledge that we have in general. The next level of awareness is knowing when and how to apply that knowledge.

Life is continually giving us feedback. It gives us feedback when we show a lack of awareness, and when it is apparent that we don't have sufficient sensitivity or, if our perspective is too narrow, to appreciate the impact of our decisions. If we are open, the world will give us feedback about the areas where we need to expand our awareness. Another way of expanding awareness is to look for role models and ask yourself, "What is it that this person is seeing that I'm missing?" Watching what they pay attention to and the kinds of questions they ask can be helpful in expanding your awareness.

Our awareness increases when we lose our sense of certainty. The more certain we are of things, the more blind spots we have, and the more likely we are to not see things as clearly as we could. Leaders who think they know everything cannot only be misguided, they also can be destructive. With increasing awareness, we lose our sense of certainty. Most of us felt we were a lot smarter at twenty than we are today. Our parents seem much smarter as we get older because we realize there is so much that we thought we knew that we didn't know. The more we learn, the more aware we are of all the things we don't know. One way of expanding your field of vision is to lose your sense of certainty.

As we noted earlier, you can change your field of vision by changing your vantage point. You can also narrow or expand your field of vision by shifting back and forth between foreground and background. But field of vision is also affected by your state of mind. If you're in a frenetic state or continually shifting your focus, you can miss the bigger picture. There are times when you need to center yourself to really *see the field*.

There's a poignant scene in the movie *The Legend of Bagger Vance* where Bagger tells Rannulph, the fellow he's caddying for, "See the field." In this case, seeing the field means focusing on what's important and then ruling out those things that are extraneous. The irony is that, to expand your field of awareness, you have to both focus on and rule out things simultaneously.

SOME INDICATORS OF AWARENESS

We know an empowering leader, who, when he's with people who are highly aware, is either surprised by the questions they ask or by the observations they make. He responds, "Hm . . . I didn't see that. That's an interesting question. That makes me look at things in a different way." So there's an element of being surprised, of recognizing that, "Gee, I didn't see that thing in the refrigerator that was sitting right there," or, "I didn't see that possibility or that way forward."

It's interesting how the really brilliant ideas are at times the most obvious. But it wasn't obvious until someone pointed it out. Up until that point, no one got it. But the person who did was keenly aware. One indicator of awareness is being surprised by the insight that someone is offering. At times we surprise ourselves. When we become aware of something we've been missing we get a visceral feeling of *a-ha!*

When you have learned a new way of looking at things and can actually see in that new way, it gives you a sense of accomplishment or a good feeling. Now, after spending time in the woods with a naturalist, when one of us walks in the woods and sees a particular berry, he knows it is edible. He used to walk past that berry bush and not even know it was there. With increased awareness, it is as though, as an empowering leader, you have a new lens or this set of lenses that reveal things which previously were virtually invisible to you. When your awareness expands it is easier to know when you are headed in the right direction, making progress, or actually seeing in a way that you couldn't see before.

Another indicator of increased awareness is that we end up behaving better as human beings. Our behavior improves as a result of awareness. We don't do things that we may have done previously when we were less aware. We don't do things to other people that might be hurtful. We don't behave in self-destructive ways as much. We don't often take wrong paths. Increased awareness leads to solutions and improved behavior. We know someone who is generally kinder now, as a person, than he was five or ten years ago because he had life experiences that made him feel the need for kindness. Now he is more aware of that need in others.

As an empowering leader, you are a highly visible person in your organization. You have to come to grips with the fact that people perceive you in a certain way that may not match your own self-perception, or, they look for clues from you and magnify those clues. Your self-awareness has to expand enough for you to know that you've got to behave in certain ways because you're not just behaving for yourself anymore. You are behaving for others too. It becomes necessary for you to pick up on the signals from other people more quickly. You become the fish in the fishbowl where everything is magnified to those looking at you.

AWARENESS INVOLVES BOTH SEEING AND UNDERSTANDING

Awareness requires both the act of seeing and also being the seer. It's both taking in the information and processing it. It's certainly not enough to just see something without putting it into some context that requires understanding. People who are very bright may have a high level of intellectual awareness, but they may not have a high level of emotional awareness or aesthetic awareness. As an empowering leader, you need many different kinds of awareness. You need to be intellectually aware, emotionally aware, and aesthetically aware. There are times you may need to be kinesthetically aware and be physically present to get the actual physical feel of a situation.

Regardless of the type of awareness, it exists on a continuum from being unaware (a lack of awareness), to the other end of being completely aware. Buddhists strive to be completely aware; they call it *clear seeing*. We can think about awareness as another type of intelligence, something that we can develop and continually expand, refine, and cultivate.

Expanding our awareness means being more *aware of what*, and *aware of how*, and *aware of why* with respect to the circumstances confronting us. There is a remarkable overlay between enlightened, empowering leadership and high levels of awareness. The more we are aware, the more we can see what's right, and the more we'll know how to do what's right, and the more we'll know that we are doing it for the right reasons.

TO BECOME A MORE EMPOWERING LEADER

- Know why awareness is an important core value.
- Know why it is important to become more self-aware.

- Know there are lenses of awareness that are especially useful.
- Expand your repertoire of lenses of awareness.
- Try to see from multiple vantage points.
- Expand your awareness and field of vision.
- Know some indicators of awareness.
- Know that awareness involves both seeing and understanding.

Core Value 11

Using Your Higher Self to Tap into Your Inner Wisdom

Are you aware that you have what we and others call a higher self? It is active when you are at your very best. It's the best version of you. It's the you that you strive to become. It's the you that whispers in your ear. It's the you that you experience when you are at peak performance. It's the you that knows what's right. It's the you that you experience when you're really sharp and on top of things. It seems to come and go. How do you get in touch with it when you need it? How do you become more attuned to its guidance? How can you use it to expand your power? How can you use it to tap into your inner wisdom?

OUR HIGHER SELF

There are two levels or aspects to our higher self. There's the level that is part of us, the best part of who we really are, and then there's a level above that, where we rise above our limitations as human beings to the more ethereal part of us that is divine. In this context, by "divine" we mean an aspect of our consciousness that is connected to a universal or transpersonal consciousness.

Our higher self is that little voice inside of us that knows what's right in all circumstances. As human beings, we get very confused by the events around us and often we're not sure what the right course of action is in any given situation. But our higher self isn't confused. Our higher self always knows what's right. From that point of view, we can think of it as our potential best friend. It's an aspect of us that is available to guide us and help us navigate through the vicissitudes and the complexities of life.

One of the miracles of modern science is the GPS (global positioning system) available on most cars and smartphones. You just turn it on and instantly it tells you where you are so that you can't get lost. You can see where the streets are and the possible routes that will take you where you need to go. Your higher self is like a GPS system. Instead of being connected to a system of satellites, your higher self is connected to the divine and can show us where we are at any moment. And like the GPS, it will help you get to your chosen destination whether you need to get there in the next five minutes, five days, or five years. Our task is to figure out how to turn our higher-self screen on and check it periodically.

AN INNER GUIDING LIGHT

Empowering leaders have a sense that they have an inner spark, a divine spark, and that everyone else has it, too. In our mind's eye, it is seen as a spark of light. Its primary purpose is to guide us. When we allow it to guide us, it pleases that inner light. In other words, it wants to be used, and it wants to be helpful, and it wants to fulfill its mission and purpose. When we allow it to shine through we get a sense of rightness. We get a sense that we are on the right path. We get a feeling of wholeness and a feeling of connection. It's those times when all is right with the world, because we really are *in sync* with exactly what we ought to be doing at a given point in time.

Normally, we think a guiding light is something external. It is the metaphor of a lighthouse or something you see off in the distance that guides you, like the north star. But the light, which is available for guidance, is not so much outside of us as it is inside us. You don't have to wait for a cloudless night or for conditions to be right to access it because it's always within you. A lot of us miss that point. We're waiting for external events to line up to show us where we need to go rather than seeing what is there for the asking, because it's inside of us all along. The last place you look is always inside of yourself. And when you do, there's usually a pleasant surprise. Most of us spend most of our time not knowing exactly what it is we ought to be doing. When we take the time to slow things down to listen to that still, small, inner voice that speaks to us and we actually listen, we get a sense of clarity.

ENERGIZING OUR HIGHER SELF

When we follow our guiding light, it helps to energize the light itself. When we operate in accord with our higher self, in accord with the best version of who we are and with what we know at a deep level within, a self-fulfilling prophecy unfolds. There is a positive feedback loop. When you are *spot on* in following your inner light, your connection to the light is both energized and turned on more easily. It's like feeding a flame with positive energy. The more we operate in accord with our higher calling, mission, and purpose, the more we are energized by our higher self, and the more our higher self is energized.

There are many ways to energize or *feed* your higher self as well as ways of cultivating your connection to it. Some people do it through meditation. Some people do it through prayer and worship. Some people do it through contemplative study. Some people do it through energy practices such as Reiki or yoga. Some people do it through dance and mudras (a movement or pose in yoga). There is no particular right way, or only way, to feed the flame. What is common is that the flame must be fed. It takes work and commitment over time. Hope is not enough.

An additional element that can feed the connection is having an attitude of gratitude. In this context, it's gratitude for our higher self or for the wisdom of our higher self. Not only do people want to be appreciated, but the divine also responds to appreciation, including the divine spark within us.

ACCESSING OUR HIGHER SELF

Others may call it our *true self*, *real self*, or *soul consciousness*. We prefer the term *higher self*. There are many techniques for accessing the higher self, including: meditation, prayer, chanting, and ritualized dance. As with most things in life, these techniques can be practiced at a beginner's level or at very advanced levels.

At a beginner's level, you might try the following: Close your eyes. Place yourself in a peaceful and quiet setting. Sit quietly for a minute or so. Breathe deeply through your nose and exhale out of your mouth. Be conscious of your breathing. Now, in your mind or by sub-vocalizing, ask your higher self for guidance. The guidance can come in different forms. It can be a moment of insight, intuition or clarity. It can come in a dream or through synchronicity (see bonus chapter 1).

Reiki, a healing art, can also be used as a direct means of connecting with your own higher self or with the higher self of another being. There are other traditions that utilize guided meditation, visualization, focused prayer, mantras (a word, sound, or phrase repeated to aid in meditation), and mudras (a movement or pose in yoga) to connect to one's higher self.

Of course, any discussion about accessing your higher self presupposes you believe you have one. It's really hard to access something if you don't think it's there. If you believe it is, that's the beginning of the process. It is then that you can chart a path on how best to tap into it. There are a remark-able number of people in the world who don't have any awareness that they have a higher self. They don't see the possibilities of having a personal GPS system available. They are just trying to find their way through uncharted terrain without a higher view.

LISTENING TO OUR HIGHER SELF

In the romantic comedy *Fools Rush In*, there are hilarious unresolved rela-tionship issues between Isabel, played by Salma Hayek, and Alex, played by Matthew Perry. In the movie, there are signs everywhere that could guide him. Finally, when he opens up, Alex sees pictures on the sides of buses; he sees people on the street; he hears words that all connect to his relationship. He finally tunes into the fact that there are signs everywhere revealing the answer to the question he has been struggling with. In part, listening to our higher self is knowing that the way the guidance comes to us is not going to be a boom-ing announcement over the loudspeaker system. It's going to be picking up on what seem to be coincidences, or interesting connections that you don't expect to find, and being open and attuned to what is being presented to you.

The signs are going to come in many different forms, and it won't neces-sarily be a voice guiding you. Some people get voices or images or something very similar where the clarity is pretty obvious. But in other cases, be aware that you may be getting the confirmation that you need through a variety of channels and a variety of sources. A sense of openness is required to consider all the things coming at you and to consider which of them you need to pay attention to.

Listening to our higher self is both an internal and an external process. There is listening when we've asked a question. That is, we may ask a ques-tion of our higher self, or we may ask for support, help, or specific guidance from our higher self. And once we've done that, we should be especially at-tuned for the answers to show up, sometimes in surprising forms. At times, our higher self sends us messages that we may not have asked for. It's trying to get our attention. That requires a tougher kind of listening.

A lot of what we get is guidance we don't ask for because the notion of a higher self is that the higher self knows what we need to know, even though we may not know that we need to know it. The higher self is always at work. It's working even when you don't ask it to. It's telling you things you prob-ably don't *want* to hear but that you *need* to hear.

Which brings us back to the issue of openness and acceptance, knowing that part of listening is to accept that you may be getting messages which may not be entirely welcome in your life because it interferes with what you are doing or planning to do. Your actions or plans may be wrong for you. Perhaps what you're asking for is not good for you. Perhaps you should be paying attention to some other issues. In some areas of our lives, guidance keeps coming at you, whether you asked for it or not. You'll continue to get those messages until you *get it* or suffer the consequences.

The higher self is a more benign deliverer of messages than the world at large. It's tapping you on the shoulder and saying, "Hey, pay attention. Here's a thought. Have you considered?" There's gentleness to the higher self that the world at large doesn't give you because it is part of who you are. It doesn't want to see you hurt. It is constantly asking you to pay attention and to tune in, but if you don't, ultimately you're probably going to pay a price.

OUR CONNECTION TO OTHERS

An empowering leader of a national organization told us about a time he was getting prepared for a national conference. He knew he needed to go out onstage and communicate with thousands of people. He wanted those in attendance to understand the importance of what he was saying. He discussed his concern with a friend who was highly intuitive. His friend said, "Why don't you have a meeting of your higher self and the higher selves of all the people that are going to be there tomorrow? Call them all together in your mind. Have your higher self deliver a message that you really need them to listen to what you'll be saying and why." So he did it. He actually tried doing just that.

Afterward, he said it was incredibly powerful because there was a sense of something else operating in the room beside the words that he was saying. He used the types of words and phrases and intonation and gestures he had always used when onstage talking to large groups of people, but he had a sense that there was some other connection going on that was much more powerful than usual. He felt he had connected, higher self to higher self, with everyone in the room.

This empowering leader, with some advice from his intuitive friend, stumbled upon the power of intention to connect with others at the level of higher self. As an empowering leader, you say something like, "It is my intention to reach out and to connect with the higher selves or the divine aspects of all the people who are going to be in this room or all the people throughout the country who are interested in this particular issue." And you state your intention. Our higher self is not bound by time and space because the communication takes place at the quantum level of reality. We mentioned earlier that Reiki was one of the healing arts that could be used to connect your higher self to the higher self of another individual. At more advanced levels, Reiki techniques can connect your higher self to the higher selves of any group of individuals, anywhere at anytime, now or in the future.

We've been talking about the higher self, which by definition is ethereal. Here is a metaphor that may be helpful in bringing it into clearer focus. Imagine going to your high school prom. You may get dressed up in a tuxedo, your hair combed, and you look like a prince. You may get dressed up in a gown, your hair made up, and you look like a princess. It's presenting yourself to the world looking your very best. And when you get to the prom, everyone dances and enjoys being together. That's how your higher self connects to others; everybody is really going to a black tie affair for the soul. When you do higher-self-to-higher-self communication, it's the best part of you connecting to the best part of other people.

It is not your nasty, ugly self. It is not your sloppy, awful self. It's you putting on your best possible persona and connecting to their best possible persona. The power is really about connecting at that best place that each of you has to offer, because it's pure, and it's not bogged down by the weight of greed, selfishness, and other self-serving things. It's light and positive and spiffed up. It's the best part of you connected to the best part of them. When you get dressed up to go to the ball, you're not only looking good yourself, you're also seeing other people at their best. You are respecting each other by dressing up for the occasion and acting in a courtly manner.

OUR POWER EXPANDS WHEN WE ACT AND
SPEAK IN ACCORDANCE WITH OUR HIGHER SELF

Empowering leaders have integrity and work at being integrated. The ultimate in integration is when our thoughts, words, and actions are in alignment with our best purposes and our highest sense of who we are. When this occurs, you have a sense of power and thrust in what you do. You're energized and able to move forward. When you're in alignment it brings clarity to what you're about. You bring a sense of honor to the people you are dealing with. When you are out of alignment, it's like when your car is out of alignment. It wobbles. It pulls to the right. It pulls to the left. You have to fight it to get it to go where it needs to go. There is a struggle.

When you are in alignment, there is no struggle. You're able to go straight. You're able to move forward with a sense of power and authority. That makes you more effective as a person and as a leader. When your thoughts, actions, and words are aligned with what your higher self is guiding you to do, it is incredibly powerful. Generally, the higher self pushes us toward service and toward carrying out a mission that is bigger than ourselves. When you do that, you tend to have a little more oomph behind what you're doing than when you're just doing it for yourself.

Leaders generally want more power and want to be more powerful. One of the ways of acquiring additional power is alignment with your higher self, because the more aligned you are, the more power comes into you. While it is true that the ultimate occurs when what you think, say, and do line up, any one of those can also be aligned with your higher self. Every time that happens, there is an increase in power. This also increases your power to attract. When you are aligned with your higher self, other people are attracted to you, your ideas, and your initiatives. That is why it feels powerful, because the power is actually being derived from all of the other individuals who are aligning themselves with you as a result of the energy that is being emitted. You are finding power with people, not exerting power over them.

BEING FULL OF POWER AS OPPOSED TO BEING POWERFUL

Have you ever thought about how being full of power differs from being powerful? The former is earned while the latter is conferred. One is internal and one is external. If you are powerful, it has been conferred upon you. You've been elected to it, appointed to it, or usurped it. You've done something that has put you in a position of having power over other people, and that is external. What can be given can be taken away. We see that in politics. We see that in the military. We see that in the corporate world. So when you are powerful, it is conditional and external.

When you are full of power and maintain that sense of being full of power, it is not conditional. It is something that you have given yourself through your actions, your connection to your higher self, and to your alignment and attunement to your purpose. When you are full of power, it comes from internal sources. It comes from your connections. It comes from who and what you are as a person, not what you do or the title that you hold. Your job is what you do; it is not who you are. You should never mix up what you do with who you are. What you do could change, but who you are is who you are. That's what you take with you from one job to the next. Being full of power is knowing who you are. And being powerful is knowing what you are. And those are two very different things.

Martin Luther King Jr., a Baptist minister and civil rights activist, was assassinated in 1968, but his power has radiated beyond his lifetime. People are still talking about his vision, still talking about his dreams, and still talking about his hopes for the world. Here was a man who was full of power.

When you are full of power, you are almost unassailable, because what you have can't be taken from you. The more fully in touch you are with your higher self the more you will find that you are full of power.

OUR HIGHER SELF ENDEAVORS
TO GUIDE US TO DO OUR BEST

Let's try a thought experiment. Imagine what it would be like to be in the place of your higher self. Wouldn't it be frustrated most of the time? It would be giving you its constant attention. It wants you to do your best, to rise to the occasion, to be full of power, and to be on the right side of things. And your lower self is always working against that. The lower self wins a lot of the times. It must be very frustrating for the higher self to put up with that. That's real unconditional love, for it to keep coming back and offering the best course of action when most of the time we ignore it. It's like we know what we should eat, we know what we should be doing, but we don't do it. That chocolate pie looks really good. "I think I'll just have a piece of that, even though I know I shouldn't." Metaphorically, we spend a lot of time in our lives eating chocolate pie.

The metaphorical piece of chocolate pie is always calling to us. What is it that helps us at times to say no or just take a small bite or even choose a piece of fruit instead? What is it within that encourages us, supports us, and pushes us in the direction of doing our best? We say it is our internal navigating system that we call our higher self. No matter how often we ignore it, the amazing thing is it always keeps coming back and keeps pushing. We might have given up on ourselves long ago, but the nice thing is that our higher self never quits, and that's pretty remarkable. It's hard work to keep pushing against those lower, more selfish, self-indulgent parts of who we are. It is relentless in trying to get us to do the right thing, and to support that in terms of its guidance.

Here is a ditty that may help remind you to treat yourself the way your higher self does: *Good better best. Never let it rest until the good is better, and the better is best.*

OUR HIGHER SELF HELPS US TO BECOME
BETTER VERSIONS OF OURSELVES

Most of us strive to become better at what we do and to become better people over time. Clearly, we human beings are a work in progress. We are reminded of the sign once spotted in a shop that reads: *Be patient. God's not done with me yet.* Human beings are capable of growing and evolving and, at the very least, it is a lifelong process. Many people think the process of becoming better and better versions ourselves may even be a multi-lifetime process.

When you realize that we are all works in progress, it should help you to be patient with yourself and to be patient with others. At best, this process is two steps forward and one step back, and at times it's one step forward and two steps back. It is an ongoing process with fits and starts but the ultimate trajectory is to try to move us toward the best versions of who and what we can be. That's the role of our higher self, and when we understand this, we can be more empowering to others because we understand they are on their own journey to a better self as well.

Our higher self also helps us fight against the worst versions of ourselves. If it weren't for the struggle between these different aspects of ourselves, we might not make progress. We might not have the chance to move the ball forward or get ourselves cleaned up to present ourselves in the best light.

We live in an age where the operating systems of our computers and smartphones continually receive upgrades. That's what our higher self endeavors to do for us.

OUR HIGHER SELF HELPS US TO
BECOME WHO WE REALLY ARE

Who knows what you are capable of? Empowering leaders build solid floors for people to stand on but no ceilings overhead because they don't know the heights to which people can soar. Our higher self can't make us into someone we're not, but we are all capable of much more than we typically show. We're all capable of becoming much more of who we are and who we can become. Our higher self helps us find that place where we can become more and more of who we are.

We are all given gifts. The gifts are different, but we're all given them. There are extraordinarily gifted people like Martin Luther King Jr. or Gandhi who took the gifts they were given and magnified them in the service of others. Our higher self is always suggesting we have important gifts *too*. As empowering leaders, we have a dual obligation. One is for us to do everything we can to make as much of ourselves as possible, and the other is to provide an atmosphere and a support system for the people around us to have that same opportunity. Our higher self points the way.

Our jobs are what we do, but they're not who we are. That begs the questions: "Who are we?" And "Who knows who we are?" We believe it is that higher self that really knows who we are, deep down at our core. As we act in the world, some times we operate in accord with that and some times we don't. There are times we say, "What was I thinking?" There are times we say, "This is not who I am. What I just said, or what I just did; this isn't me. I mean, Yes, I did it, but I'm remorseful about it. I'm embarrassed by it. I'm uncomfortable about it. It just doesn't feel right. Upon reflection, I reject it. It's not me." It's the spark from your higher self that is constantly giving you the template from the real you that helps you make that assessment.

Over time, through our experiences and life lessons, our higher self guides us toward our highest and best destiny.

EMPOWERING LEADERS

- Know that they have a higher self.
- See their higher self as an inner guiding light.
- Can access their higher self.
- Know how to listen to their higher self.
- Know our higher self can connect us to others.
- Know our power expands when we act in accord with our higher self.
- Know our power expands when we speak in accord with our higher self.
- Know our higher self is a source of power.
- Know our higher self guides us to do our best.
- Know our higher self helps us become better versions of ourselves.
- Know our higher self helps us become who we really are.

Using Openness to Expand Possibilities

Empowering leaders understand and recognize the power of openness for effective leadership. Openness is an attitude that allows the best possibilities to emerge from the individuals in the organization and from the organizations themselves. Closed minds and systems lead to stagnation and a withering of potential. When you are open, you see, hear, and experience things that raise questions or lead to possibilities.

Empowering leaders foster openness by modeling it. They show their open heart and mind, and they demonstrate that openness by accepting that value in others. They create a climate and culture where people feel free to express their ideas, feelings, and creativity. They create an atmosphere where people feel respected and trusted and where there is open, two-way communication. They set up opportunities for collaboration. Empowering leaders understand that openness is the key for growth.

Empowering leaders understand that meaning and purpose are central to every life and organization. They aspire to making things better. They see the best in others and seek to cultivate the qualities in themselves and others that enhance the quality of life. By being open to the infinite potential in themselves and others, empowering leaders help those around them to tap into their potential to create and find fulfillment.

OPENNESS IS A CORE VALUE
FOR EMPOWERING LEADERS

Throughout this book, we have talked about openness in various ways. It seems to be a prerequisite to so many of the values we have discussed. It allows the other values we have mentioned to come forward. Although it seems so fundamental, it is interesting to note how people fall across a wide continuum when it comes to openness.

When you allow things into your life, it enriches it. When you are closed off to possibilities, you lose the chance for magic to happen. Openness is a prerequisite for a fulfilled life, but it is just as critical for an organization because the lack of openness harms the dynamics of an organization and makes the organization unhealthy.

The question an empowering leader must ask is this: "Openness to what?" To answer that question requires openness itself because the answers are so vast: openness to life experiences, openness to ideas, openness to being known by others, openness to change, to criticism, to growth. Openness is qualitative. Are you open? But it is also quantitative. How open are you? To what extent are you open or will you be open?

It is important to note that openness is a continuum and it also varies area to area. You might be very open in your life choices but closed off in your openness to new ideas. You might see this topic as a room with many doors and they are each open to a greater or lesser degree. The empowering leader remembers that you cannot go through a door unless it is open.

Since we never know what is on the other side of the door—the lady or the tiger—being open requires courage. You have to be willing to step into the unknown and walk into a room you might not imagine. Openness encompasses the issues of fear and trust. You cannot be fearful and open. You cannot be trusting and closed. When things are closed, nothing flows.

We know from health that blockages are dangerous. A blockage in your blood flow creates catastrophic effects. A blockage in your airflow will kill you quickly. Organizations cannot survive blockages in the flow of energy, ideas, and creativity required for success. Blocked organizations wither and die.

For organizations to be open, leaders must model that behavior. They must demonstrate their openness to ideas, criticism, and expansion. They must be courageous enough to walk through doors that lead to unknown places.

Creative leaders must be open. Now, more than ever, the world needs creative and courageous leaders. Leaders must be able to access everything that is available and be willing to make things available that might not be obvious at first glance. The essence of creativity is discovering the connections between what is seen and what is unseen. It is finding new connections between disparate ideas. The power of creativity is saying or doing something that, once it is done, everyone sees how obvious it was in the first place.

THE HIGHER ASPECTS OF OPENNESS

Openness requires a certain degree of trust and hope, which are fundamental values of leadership. You have to have a belief or hope that things will come to you and your organization that will benefit the work. And you have to trust the process to allow that to happen. Great leaders make decisions or take actions that others with lesser belief and hope might question. We believe that the universe is not simply a random place where good or bad are indistinguishable. We believe the universe works toward good outcomes. As Martin Luther King Jr. put it, "The arc of the moral universe is long, but it bends toward justice."

Belief in a higher power will not ensure openness. We have seen many people who espouse their beliefs but who operate with a closed mind and heart. Consider the idea that the enemy of openness is orthodoxy. The issue here is whether you are open to other ideas or whether these ideas create judgment in you. You deem them right or wrong. If you can accept the idea that someone else may think differently than you but still be right, you are on the path to openness.

We believe that each of us holds a spark of the divine. If that is true, then openness toward that spark of goodness in others is mandatory. This all may seem strange territory for a hard-nosed leader to consider, but we believe it is fundamental to the ability to be open and to promote it.

The more boundaries you create, the more structured you become, and the more rules you lay down, the more you move away from openness. Certainly, any organization requires some rules and parameters, but the less you trust those around you, the more boundaries you will create. The key is to have only the rules necessary for the organization to function and for those in it to do their work. Empowering leaders must use their sense of faith and trust to create the rules of opportunity for the organization.

EMPOWERING LEADERS CREATE OPEN SYSTEMS

Throughout this book, we have pointed out that to incorporate the values we have presented into the organization first requires the leader to model these values. This is no less true for the value of openness. Further, the leader must create ways for those in the organization to grow and experience each other in new and positive ways.

Peters and Waterman, in their classic management book *In Search of Excellence*, suggested that leaders had to be tight on the goals and loose on the ways to achieve them. You have to be clear on where you want the organization to go, but you have to be open to and offer a lot of options for getting there.

According to systems theory, open systems create a feedback loop. Information goes out into the system and then comes back, and then there is a form of reaction and adjustment, and then it goes out again. There is a continual flow of information through open communication and the flow of information is in two directions.

Empowering leaders create systems for two-way communication. Too many organizations only operate one way, and they create barriers for the flow of information. Leaders in these organizations cannot be considered empowering. Leaders can give people experiences that will allow them to become more open. The more open the people become, the more open the system is.

There is a program in more and more schools called "service learning," which involves high school students working in the community in service to others. One such program involved high school students working with the elderly in nursing homes. The students started the process with many misconceptions about the elderly. It was also true that the elderly had many mistaken ideas about the young people of today. Through their work together, they both learned and grew and understood each other better.

Sometimes helping people grow requires throwing them a safety line. We have all had experiences with talented people who grew very comfortable in their roles. When offered positions of more responsibility, they decline the offer. The leader can let them stay content or can challenge them to grow, but the challenge should be accompanied by a safety line. They might be told if they were uncomfortable, they could return to their previous role, or they may be offered specific kinds of support to make certain they feel supported and successful. Usually, they will find the new role even more rewarding than the one they were reluctant to abandon.

Sometimes when you are making a change, you have to give people an opportunity to talk with and spend time with people who have already experienced the change that you are suggesting. We know a principal who was trying to introduce a different kind of schedule in a high school. He let the teachers spend time with teachers in a different setting who were already following the new schedule. They then became more open to the change.

It is also important for an organization to have new blood from time to time. It is not bad to have to deal with people who might be different from you. They bring new and different perspectives, and they help you grow. History tells us about the upheaval and ultimate success of Truman integrating the army shortly after World War II. It is hard now to imagine what a radical idea it was at the time.

More recently, we have seen the results of Title IX. This was a law enacted in the 1980s that required schools and universities to provide equal services for women in athletics. At the time, it was controversial, and it challenged the institutions to comply. More recently, we have seen the fruits of that effort as America's women athletes have dominated international competition.

It has often been suggested that you can lead a horse to water, but you can't make him drink. The reality is that all you have to do is make sure the horse is thirsty, and he will decide to drink on his own.

EMPOWERING LEADERS MUST
BE OPEN TO MANY THINGS

The first thing an empowering leader needs to be open to is change. People like to say that the only things that are certain are death and taxes, but it is pretty clear that change ought to be added to that list. The universe is a dynamic and constantly changing place. Whether you are looking at the cellular level or the galactic level, what is constant is change. While the rate and degree of change varies, change is always with us so we better be open to it.

When an organization has an open culture, people are encouraged to come forward with new ideas and initiatives. An empowering leader remains open to considering the ideas and suggestions and concerns that come forward. Further, an empowering leader makes certain that the climate of the organization encourages this dynamic.

We must be open to the information that comes to us. Not everything we might hear or face will be pleasant. Change can challenge our very core. As leaders, we have to be open to hearing and seeing the good and the bad. We have had times when someone tells us something that is disturbing, but later we found that by having that information, it ultimately benefitted us. When we are not open to the vicissitudes that face us we miss the good and the bad. There is an old line from *Star Trek* that suggests that resistance is futile. When it comes to change, that is spot on, and an empowering leader understands and uses change to her benefit.

Often it is difficult to embrace the pain of change. For example, someone we know has a fear of crossing bridges. It has been suggested that it is a phobia, but it may not be. Phobias are irrational fears, but there is nothing irrational about crossing from a place you know, which may be a place of safety, to a place you don't know that might be dangerous. But, ultimately, leadership is really about crossing bridges and taking your people with you.

Sometimes you have to face the pain of new ideas, of rejection, of being knocked off your pedestal. But you have to stay open to other people—to their ideas, their criticism, and their being in your space. Empowering leaders have to be open to learning to play well with others.

We also have to be open to the paradoxical nature of life. We have to understand that two and two doesn't always make four. It depends on the numerical system being used. There are no right or wrong answers to some problems. Sometimes success is preventing something from getting worse. It is often hard to know the right path because there is no right path. Sometimes there isn't even a path!

Most of the time, as a leader, you are just cutting your way through the underbrush, hoping to find your way. Sometimes you choose the right direction and you get where you want to go quickly and efficiently, and sometimes you are just on a scenic route to nowhere. But when you take the scenic route, you see things you never imagined. You have to be open to the surprise and magic that is out there.

Yogi Berra once said, "You can observe a lot just by watching." You can also hear a lot by listening. You have to be open to what you see and hear and be ready to adjust and respond. Wonderful things sometime happen unexpectedly, but so do awful things. You have to learn to adjust. Sometimes when you get to the place you wanted to go, you realize it was just the beginning point for your next journey. Life and leadership are messy endeavors, and empowering leaders are open to that insight.

Perhaps more important than even keeping your eyes and ears open is the need to keep your heart open. This will open more channels of possibility. When we open all aspects of our being, the world opens up for us. We also need to be aware that openness is a transitory thing. Sometimes we are more open than others. We have to monitor how open we are on an ongoing basis. Time and circumstances change us and we have to adjust.

Think of a door that doesn't hang quite level. It can be open, but it gradually swings shut. We have to maintain our clarity so that we can take in what is being offered. The paradox of openness is staying open to the knowledge that you are not always going to be open.

Openness is not linear where you get a little more open each year. It moves back and forth and the key is to tune into your openness and make adjustments. Our heart valves open and close and so do our minds. The work of openness is an ongoing challenge because things will push you to be more closed off. Being closed is a form of self-protection, but it doesn't really work in the long run. When you keep a thick shell someone is always going to want to test its thickness. Sometimes your greatest strength is to remain open and vulnerable.

OPENING YOUR HEART AND MIND

Is it possible to have an open mind if your heart is closed? Can you have an open heart if your mind is closed? We don't think either of these things is possible. Sometimes your heart must understand what you mind cannot comprehend. When we are part of a tragedy or we lose a loved one or a love, it is our heart that must first comprehend what is happening. Our minds may never catch up.

Minds are a cluttered place. We get so many pieces of information, ideas, and messages that it is often very difficult to sort them out. At best, it is confusing, and at worst, it is debilitating. Our heart is much less cluttered. It only has one job and that is to feel. The mind has the capacity to close down the heart and the heart has the ability to open the mind.

Having an open heart involves values such as trust and forgiveness. When you are an unforgiving person, you remember all the slights and hurts that others have created and you hold on to them. This makes it hard for your mind or heart to be open. Sometimes the best way to be liberated is to just let go, something easier said than done for many of us. You have to be willing to risk and to feel pain. The paradox here is that when you dwell on fear you cut yourself off from the possibility of happiness and success. You create what you most fear.

We can be proactive in opening our hearts and minds. If we want to have a heart that feels deeply, wanting that is the first step to making it real. We have to be willing to tell our mind that we want to be more open to trying new things and accepting new ideas. If you want to be healthy, you have to act on it. You can't sit around and think, "I want to be healthier." You have to get up and move and eat better and get more sleep. You have to be proactive. The same is true for having an open mind and heart.

We know of an organization that called itself "Do Something." It had a specific idea of what it wanted to do, but like the old ads for Nike—"Just Do It"—it is a pretty good reminder of getting started on opening our hearts and minds. Take an inventory of how open you are. Start to work on your closed areas. *Just do something.*

We are constantly getting feedback on how closed we are. We realize that we missed certain opportunities; people react to us in certain ways. All of these are signs. How do we choose to handle this feedback? Do we get further closed off, or do we realize we need to change? We have all known people who had physical or emotional issues that closed them off to a fuller life. Sometimes these people are open to taking small steps that will broaden their lives, but, too often, they just refuse to make a change.

One way of opening our hearts and minds is to look for people who exhibit those qualities. Then we have a role model to follow. The motivational guru Tony Robbins is known for saying that success leaves clues. Look for those who are successful at being open and search for the clues they are offering. When we are around open people, they make us feel better. We can then strive to emulate their behavior.

One powerful aspect of openness is *unconditionality*. The more conditions you put on your interactions, beliefs, or your behaviors, the more closed you become. Certainly, the goal of *unconditionality* is elusive and one we probably could never fully achieve. It is the journey toward it that sets good leaders apart from weaker ones. The key to moving in that direction is to find empathy for others. When you can put yourself in their place, you can expand your openness to them.

We know someone who is a hoarder of sorts. He collects things and holds on to them. From time to time, life gives him a jarring reminder that stuff clutters up his life. The stuff we hold onto, whether it is physical or psychological, is clutter that keeps us from feeling completely fulfilled. When you get rid of your excess baggage, you can become more open.

Openness is an action, but it is also a reaction. You can be proactive in creating openness as you take a thoughtful journey toward having an open mind and heart. But life happens, and we react. We have to stay aware so that our reactions are open. This can be even harder than having a proactive intention because we tend to be led by the things that are happening to us. When you are confronted with someone who isn't very open, it becomes far too easy to react similarly. You have to break the pattern and move in a new direction to avoid behaving the way they are behaving.

It is important to remember that growth itself is an open process. We cannot grow when our hearts and minds are closed. Sometimes it takes heartache and heartbreak to become more open. But sometimes all it takes is a whisper from someone we love or admire, or it can be something as sweet and gentle as experiencing the loving look in a child's eyes.

OPENNESS MAXIMIZES GROWTH AND CREATIVITY

When you are overloaded with baggage, it is hard to travel. We overload ourselves with biases, preconceptions, prejudices, anger, and resentment. When these things overload you, they are rocks in your pocket that weigh you down. If birds were as weighed down as we are, they would never get off the ground. When we start to remove the weight of our baggage, we allow our creativity to flourish.

If you have a lot of preconceptions about something, it doesn't allow you to see with open eyes and an open heart what is the best path for you or your organization. Sometimes we pursue a path only to learn that a different path would have been better for us. If we continue down the wrong path, we cut ourselves off from success. You have to stay open to new possibilities.

We know someone who, after being around a large group of superintendents, observed that they don't seem to be very good listeners. They tended to hold fast to their positions and tried to influence others to go along with them. This is probably true of any group of CEOs. When you are in charge, you feel as though you have to be right all the time. You think people should follow your ideas because leaders are supposed to have people follow them.

Of course, there is another choice. Robert Greenleaf, in his seminal work, *Servant Leaders*, suggested that the leader's role isn't to force people to go in the direction the leader wants. The leader's role is to serve her colleagues and staff. By serving them, you lead. When you are willing to let go of your idea that you have to be right, more creativity and growth occurs for you and your organization.

If you are a leader who worries more about control than growth, then you will lead an organization that doesn't grow and really can't go very far. Empowering leaders understand that growth is fundamental and essential for improvement. If you value growth and creativity, then you see openness as a catalyst to promoting these traits.

Staying open in our personal lives is also critical. One of our colleagues wanted to develop better eating habits to be healthier. Another wanted to cling to his Twinkies because he figured the preservatives in Twinkies would preserve him. The oatmeal boy learned to fix the oatmeal in a way that it was tasty, and he started to like it. His openness allowed him to move in a healthier direction. Twinkie boy remains closed to this possibility. The reality is that to learn a new skill or set a new direction in your life, you have to be open.

We are not open all the time about all things. There are areas where we are open and others where we are closed. The key is to work on being more open, more of the time. We need to learn to expand our circle of openness and then creativity and growth will follow.

OPENNESS IS THE KEY TO CREATING INFINITE POTENTIALITY

To reach your or your organization's potential, you have to start with openness. You can't turn on the lights unless you turn on the switch. Openness is the switch for turning on your potential. Our potentiality is infinite in countless ways. We have the potential for growth, for happiness, for success in our personal and professional life, and for our connection to others. This all starts with a willingness to be open.

One of our colleagues has traveled all over the world and has gone to many exotic and out-of-the-way places. He is often asked, "Aren't you afraid?" The answer quite simply is no. He tries to be respectful of the environment he is in and to understand what precautions he must take, but he doesn't fear the experience. He believes you have to be open to the world to understand it. And fear is the enemy of openness.

If you spend all your time building walls around you to protect yourself from the world, you will miss the possibility of living in the world. In ancient times, they tried building fortresses around their cities only to find that the walls limited their growth and couldn't protect them from Trojan horses. You can only reach your potential when you tear down your walls and open yourself up.

Seeing openness as the key to living and succeeding also reminds us that keys are made to open locks. We might consider openness as a golden key because it unlocks the potential in each of us. People who work in schools often see principals and custodians walking around with a wad of keys on their belt. It is a symbol of their authority. They alone can open the doors. But each of us has the possibility of having a single golden key that will open the world for us—the key of openness.

Certainly there are challenges in our lives and it is natural to try to mitigate them. But we must understand that we progress, not in spite of the hardships we face but because of them. If we didn't have difficult people to face and difficult situations to navigate, we might never become what we can be. Rewards come not from doing what is easy, but from doing what is difficult.

EMPOWERING LEADERS UNDERSTAND THAT THEY MUST

- See openness as a fundamental core value of leadership.
- Foster openness in themselves and others.
- Remain open to seeing divine qualities in themselves and others.
- Seek to create and support open systems.
- Remain open to others.
- Remain open to life.
- Remain open to the spiritual dimension of life.
- Strive to keep an open heart.
- Strive to keep an open mind.
- Help others open their hearts and minds.
- Use openness to foster their own growth and the growth of others.
- Use openness to foster their own creativity and the creativity of others.
- See openness as a key to creating infinite potentiality in themselves and others.

Bonus Chapter 1

The Gift of Synchronicity— Our Hidden Guidance System

There is a hidden guidance system operating in the world. It is operating in plain sight, but most people are unaware of its existence. The world-renowned psychologist Carl Jung observed this universal phenomenon and named it synchronicity. Jung found that, contrary to what most people thought, there seemed to be two types of coincidences operating in the world: those that were meaningful and those that were not. He coined the term *synchronicity* to describe those that were. Whether we are aware of it or not, our lives abound with synchronicity. Joseph Jaworski, from MIT's Center for Organizational Learning, wrote a wonderful book on this phenomenon called *Synchronicity: The Inner Path of Leadership.*

So, to be clear, here is a simple, easy-to-remember definition of synchronicity: It is a meaningful coincidence. Meaningful to whom? Meaningful to you.

UNDERSTANDING THE GIFT OF SYNCHRONICITY

Think about your life. How did you come to be who you are? How did you decide where to go to school? What to study? What you wanted to be when you grew up? Where you wanted to live? Did you want to be single or get married? What kind of partner did you want, if any? Did you want to have children? Would you practice a religion? Would you be spiritual? Would you play an instrument? What sports would you play? What activities interested you? Who would you choose as your friends? Who would choose you as their friends? Who would you choose as role models? Would you be part of a political party? What organizations would you join? What goals would you set for yourself? This list goes on and on. It is our contention that unbeknownst to you, synchronicity played a role in each and every one of your life choices in ways large and small.

Your worldview affects the way you view all of these types of questions. You may believe that life is a series of chance encounters and circumstances. Cards are dealt, and you play them as well as you can. You try to learn how to be a good player, and sometimes you win and sometimes you lose. On one hand, you believe life is random and essentially it is a game of chance. On the other hand, if you believe in synchronicity, as we do, you believe that there are patterns and energies that you can attract and create. If you believe in synchronicity, you believe that life is not random, that some things happen for a reason, and some paths open to you for a reason. We encourage you to stay open to the possibility that there are forces operating in the world beyond chance.

There is an ongoing interplay between each of us and the universe. Perhaps this metaphor would be a useful way of thinking about it: There are trillions of cells in the human body, each with a purpose, and each contributing to the whole. At the start, each cell is undifferentiated and has infinite potential. Eventually, in a mysterious way, each cell chooses a path or a preferred path is chosen for it. The cell needs things from the body to function optimally, and the body needs each cell to function in certain ways for it to function optimally. There is a symbiotic relationship. Think of each of us as a cell and the universe as the body. Synchronicity is the mechanism by which we send signals to the universe for what we want. It is also the mechanism by which the universe supports us in achieving our potential.

What does this have to do with empowering leadership? There are powers at work that attract you to people and people to you, that attract you to situations, and that bring things together. When you send out energy in your thoughts, words, and deeds through synchronicity, what is needed comes into play. Leaders who are attuned to the synchronicity of events and people can create better organizations and better lives for themselves and the people around them.

MEANINGFUL COINCIDENCES
HELP SHAPE OUR FUTURE

David and Larry barely knew each other as new superintendents in 1977. Over the years, they came to know each other well, wrote books together, and became founding partners of a leadership development organization—all due to synchronicity! They came to New Jersey in the same year in neighboring counties. Larry's assistant superintendent knew David from church and took it upon himself to introduce them. David and Larry would bump into each other at education-related events during the next few years but didn't seem to have any special connection.

From today's vantage point, after countless hours of conversation and dialogue, Larry believes that his life's work (purpose) and David's were intertwined. But given their casual meeting in the late 1970s, how was this possibility to unfold? Unbeknownst to Larry, in the early to mid-1980s, as a Harvard alumnus, David started attending Harvard's seminar for superintendents. Looking back, one possibility would have been for Larry to meet David at Harvard, but what were the chances of that happening? Larry had done his doctoral work at Temple University and wasn't even aware of Harvard's summer program—until synchronicity intervened.

Then three things happened within a few months of each other. First, Larry's new high school principal (who had a master's degree from Harvard) attended Harvard's Principals Center. When he came back he not only raved about the program but told Larry about Harvard's summer program for superintendents. He knew the program director and offered to call him on Larry's behalf to secure an invitation. Larry said, "Let me think about it."

Second, Larry was talking with a respected colleague about his career aspirations and his interest in continuing his own professional growth. When Larry mentioned the program at Harvard, his colleague said immediately, "What are you waiting for? It would be perfect for you." Again Larry said, "I'll think about it."

Finally, out of the blue, Larry was invited to go on a VIP tour of NORAD in Colorado Springs. Sitting next to Larry on the plane was a superintendent from another state. Not long into the flight, he began telling Larry that he had attended Harvard's summer program for superintendents. He said the program was phenomenal and strongly recommended that Larry apply.

That was enough for Larry. From his perspective, three times the universe had sent him a message. It was time to act. When he returned, he asked his high school principal to call the contact at Harvard. David and Larry spent the next fifteen summers at Harvard exploring the ideas that would become the foundation for the book series they are writing on values-based leadership. A meaningful coincidence was set up many, many years ago to create a potentiality. It didn't mean that the future was ordained. It didn't mean they were destined to go to Harvard in the summer to connect with each other to realize that they wanted to collaborate on a series of books. It simply meant that the circumstances had been *set up* for that potentiality to manifest.

Think back on your life. How did you meet your life partner, choose your career path, or the schools you went to? You will find the synchronistic patterns that opened doors, created opportunities, and formed the basis for these potentials to unfold. When we see enough of those patterns in our own lives, we will have reason to expect that they don't just happen without reason. They are happening in real time from here forward as well. The only way you can see them is by being open to the synchronicities around you.

MEANINGFUL COINCIDENCES HELP US TO FULFILL OUR LIFE'S PURPOSES(S)

There are things that happen to us that, at the time, we fail to understand their connection to our life's purpose. But they open doors; they create connections; they start something flowing that leads to something significant, either in the short term or the long term. Yet at the moment, you could never have predicted what it was going to be or where it would lead.

Some people have a sense of their life's purpose. When events or people come into their lives that help move them forward, it's easier for them to see a pattern. If you're not sure of your life's purpose, it's less clear how the meaningful coincidences you are experiencing are helping to shape your future. It's important to pay attention to your intuition and be receptive to its signals. When something strikes you as a coincidence because an unusual pattern occurs, ask the questions, "I wonder if there is something meaningful here for me? I wonder if there is some information here that could be helpful to me? I wonder if there is something here that is giving me an opportunity to help another person in a way that is meaningful to them?" The process of synchronicity works in more than one direction.

We have to be careful about not defining our own purpose or sense of mission too narrowly. There is a fine balance between having a sense of purpose, which we think we should all have, and being so prescriptive to it that we don't open ourselves up to the other possible paths that we could be taking.

We know someone who thought the job he held was his purpose. This person struggled when that particular job had run its course. This job was perfectly suited to his skills; he liked it and was good at it, but circumstances changed politically, and it became clear that it was time to move on. He was finally able to let go when he realized his real purpose was to serve others. It wasn't a particular job that was his purpose; it was larger than that. Once he understood that, he was able to take advantage of the synchronicities that opened, showing him new and exciting possibilities for his true purpose: service.

There's wisdom in the adage, "When one door closes another opens," but only if you pay attention to the synchronicities that are presented at the time. Openness is a key in this process. Life serves up possibilities for us and doors open. We have to be open enough and receptive enough to step through, or at least peek through, or the new opportunities won't help us fulfill our life's purpose.

Here's a funny image to reinforce this point. Former pro wrestler The Rock had a signature line to the crowd: "Can you smell what The Rock is 'cookin'?" So we ask you, "Can you smell what life is cooking?" Life is always preparing meals for you, but if you're not open to the smell or to what is being served, you can go hungry. You can be surrounded by food that is extremely nourishing and still go hungry because you haven't been open to what life is cooking.

INCREASING OUR AWARENESS OF SYNCHRONICITY

Synchronicities can be dramatic and vivid, or they can be mundane and subtle. We have to develop the capacity to be both the participant and the observer. We have to be engaged in life but also stand outside of our self, watching. It is the *watcher* who notices the synchronicity. The part of you that is engaged is too busy to pay attention. Surprise often serves as a harbinger of synchronicity. Synchronicity is one of the ways that the universe responds to prayer or issues that you are confronting.

Suppose you need a hip replacement. Several different sources may recommend the same doctor or same hospital or same approach, all pointing you in a particular direction. You or someone you care for may be confronting cancer. Perhaps you've prayed for a return to good health and well being. Again, two or three different sources may recommend a particular book or treatment approach, several sources all suggesting the same thing. Coincidence? Yes. Meaningful? Yes. Synchronicity? Yes.

Synchronicities are a common phenomenon; in fact, they are so common that it is easy to miss them. It depends somewhat on whether you are reaching out to the universe or it is reaching out to you. If you are reaching out to the universe, you have some awareness of the issue with which you are wrestling. Then it might take the form of someone mentioning something to you yesterday about that very thing. You just read the same thing that person said in the paper this morning. A week later, the same information was in a television program you were watching. They all were talking about the issue on your mind, and they all were telling the same thing.

A synchronicity light should be flashing in your mind's eye saying, "Maybe there's something here that I need to explore further that will be helpful to me?" Again, the patterns that pop up are not always readily apparent. They can appear to be in disparate events and sequences and it is up to us to put the patterns together and follow through to check out the information.

When the synchronicity is initiated by the universe, it is usually fairly important to our health, well-being, or to our life's purpose. When doors open or close in our lives, it's a good time to look for synchronicities to point the way forward. When we encounter significant obstacles, it's a good time to look for synchronicities as to whether we are on the right or wrong path. When we have significant health issues, accidents, or traumatic events, it's a good time to look for synchronicities to point the way forward.

INCREASING SYNCHRONICITY IN OUR LIVES

The first time we hear a word or concept, it's a new experience for us. Then we hear it again and again. Once our receptors are attuned to that new word or concept, it seems to pop up more often in our lives. The very act of increasing our awareness of synchronicity plays a role in increasing synchronicity itself. That's not the only way synchronicity increases. Many aspects of our lives are subject to the *use it or lose it* principle, including synchronicity. If synchronicity is consistently knocking at your door and you never notice it, never respond, or don't acknowledge it, it tends to decrease. On the other hand, if you have a notion that there is something larger than yourself operating here and these patterns are meaningful and helpful to you, it increases the likelihood that synchronistic events and opportunities will come to you.

For people who believe in prayer, you can even pray for increased synchronicity. You can actually ask for synchronicities not only to increase but also your awareness of them.

When you are engaged in righteous ends, when you are focused on serving other people, when you are trying to do something good for another person, or when you're trying to do something good in the world to the best of your ability, during those times, synchronicities increase. Synchronistic events are more likely to occur when you are enhancing life in some way.

OUR SYNCHRONISTIC HELPERS

Did you ever have the feeling that some mysterious force in the universe was lending you a helping hand? Did you ever have the feeling there were forces at work that helped expand what you are about and helped you accomplish something important? Did you ever have the thought that some mysterious helpers kept your bacon out of the fire? The line between victory and defeat is razor thin, as is the line between success and failure. How many times in your life could events have easily gone the other way? Have you ever felt the wind at your back when you needed it or something seemed to push you out of harm's way? If you believe in a force in the universe greater than man, what role might that force play in synchronicity?

We would like to suggest two possibilities, neither of which is provable but which are both plausible depending on your worldview. The first view is for people of faith. The Bible is full of descriptions of spiritual entities, everything from archangels to angels to cherubim to seraphim. There is a whole hierarchy, a cosmic bureaucracy. What do they do? Do we, in fact, have guardian angels looking after us, assisting us? If so, who better to facilitate meaningful coincidences—synchronicities?

The other possibility is that we ourselves are driving the process. This possibility suggests that we are creative beings who don't fully understand our own power. Through the power of body (what we do), speech (what we say), and mind (what we think), we generate energy fields at three levels of reality—physical, atomic, and quantum—that synchronistically attract the people and circumstances we need to help us manifest what we envision.

What determines how successful we are in manifesting what we envision? If we are driving this process, what part of us is in the driver's seat? We are all multifaceted. At times our *ego* is in the driver's seat. At times it is our *lower self*, or what Carl Jung calls our *shadow self*. It is when our *higher self* is in the driver's seat that we get the best results in terms of attracting synchronicities.

Again, when the best part of you—your own internal higher angels, the selfless part of you, the purest part of you—is in the driver's seat, that's when you can attract the most synchronicities. That's when you send out energy patterns that serve as an attractor for *like-minded* energy patterns. It is a process that happens automatically in terms of emitting energy waves and attracting other energies that resonate with your energy signals. We discuss this in greater detail in bonus chapter 2.

EXPECTING THE UNEXPECTED

One of the things we can expect in life is the unexpected. It's the reason empowering leaders have to be agile and quick on their feet. Leaders are expected to plan. We are expected to have plans for almost everything imaginable, which reminds us of the joke, "Do you know how to make God laugh? Tell him you have a plan." Plans are essential to any organization, but there has to be sufficient flexibility and wiggle room to take advantage of the unexpected synchronicities that arise which may reveal a better way.

Take a moment to reflect back on your life. We suspect many of the best things that have ever happened to you were unexpected. Certainly we've all had unexpected challenges and difficulties as well. Hopefully, those were blessings in disguise because they gave us the opportunity to learn and grow and become better people. When things show up unexpectedly, we need to look at them carefully to see if they are part of a synchronistic pattern. The element of the unexpected is one of the things that can alert us to a possible synchronicity.

When you run into someone in a place that you didn't expect to see them, when you find a book in a place that you didn't expect it to be, when you get a call from someone that you had lost track of, or you read something that is the answer to a problem you've been trying hard to figure out, that's the time to pay attention. These are the types of countless unexpected events that alert us to the presence of synchronicity.

We are all part of someone else's synchronicity. Part of what we are doing will end up being a synchronistic event for someone else. That's the dance of creation, and we all have a part in the dance. We may not totally understand where we are on the floor at any given point in time, but we're all a part of the movement.

Larry, a superintendent mentioned earlier in this chapter, was out for a bike ride one morning as part of his exercise program. As he was riding along a car pulled over by the side of the road and someone waved so he stopped his bike. It was someone he knew, a former member of his staff. The person seemed to have a need to talk and share what he had been doing for the last several years. He was spending his time in retirement helping people who could no longer drive, bringing them meals and helping them get to the bank. Larry said to him, "Listening to you share what you're doing reminds me of what a really good person you are and how fortunate our students were to have you as their teacher."

Larry said goodbye and moved on. In the past, Larry was this person's superintendent. In this synchronistic moment, Larry had the opportunity to validate how this person was spending his retirement years. From the smile on this former teacher's face, he knew how important this chance encounter was to him.

There is a constant interplay that we as human beings have with each other. We all have our respective roles, but unbeknownst to us, we are all part of bigger interconnected patterns. We may not always understand them, but we ought to be grateful and open to synchronistic possibilities. You never know in advance if what you put out is going to mean something to someone else, any more than you never know when someone else is going to bring you the unexpected gift that you need at that moment.

It's easy to think of synchronicity from an ego-centric point of view: "What is the universe bringing to me?" But at the very least, it's equally important to think in terms of what it is you're bringing to others in the universe day-by-day, minute-by-minute.

Earlier, we talked about being aware of synchronicity in our lives. The other half of the equation is being aware of when we're bringing it to someone else. Occasionally, you'll get those moments where you'll realize that you've done something that you didn't know you were doing that was meaningful to someone else. Someone will say something to you like, "I really needed to hear that right now," "That confirms something that I've been thinking about doing," or however they might put it. You may not be sure why you said it, but, for them, that was a very important moment.

THE RULE OF TWOS OR THREES

Some synchronicities are readily apparent. For example, you're in Penn Station in New York City staring at a subway map. A stranger says, "You look confused, can I help you?" You say, "I'm trying to figure out how to get to the Weil Cornell Hospital on the Upper East Side." The stranger says, "I happen to live next door to that hospital, take the E train to 53rd and Lexington and then walk or take a cab 1.5 miles to 66th and York." What were the chances that out of 8 million people, a stranger would be standing next to you who knew the best way for you to get to your destination?

Other synchronicities require repeated signals to get your attention. When you have two points, you can draw a straight line. When a third point lands on that line you have confirmation you're headed in the right direction. When you have two or three events that take place that are clearly connected to each other, even if they appear to be random, those are messages about a direction you need to be thinking about, or a confirmation of something that is unfolding for you, or an answer to a question you've been trying to solve. These are moments of opportunity that pass by that are like the wind. You can feel the wind and you can sense it, but, after awhile, it's going to blow another way if you don't move with it.

Good sailors know how to catch the wind. They don't wait for a storm to see which way the wind is blowing. The rule of twos or threes is a way of seeing that there's a wind blowing in your life and to pick up on it. The universe tries to knock on your door more than once in different ways, but if you're not sensitive to the signals, can't see the patterns, or don't appreciate the information that's coming to you, then at a certain point that window of opportunity closes. If after two signals you're not quite sure, then really be on high alert for the third one, and if it comes, go with it. When the universe gives us direction three times in different ways, it's usually the right direction. Whether we fully appreciate it or not at the time, it is something that's either good for us or good for other people in our lives in a way that is yet to be revealed.

As an empowering leader, if you see a pattern of three events pointing in the same direction, it's a safe bet that you are being shown the path you should take.

TO BECOME A MORE EMPOWERING LEADER

- Understand that synchronicity is gift.
- Know that meaningful coincidences help shape our future.
- Be aware that meaningful coincidences help us to fulfill our life's purpose(s).
- Increase your awareness of synchronicity.
- Be proactive in increasing synchronicity in your life.
- Call upon your synchronistic helpers.
- Look for synchronicity in the unexpected.
- Use the rule of twos or threes to alert you to synchronicities.

Bonus Chapter 2

The Gift of Syntropy—
Constructive Action

We suspect only a handful of leaders have ever come across the term *syntropy*. Some of us may remember its counterpart, *entropy*, from our high school science classes. There are many ways of viewing entropy, but essentially it is that systems tend to move toward a state of low energy and disorder over time. There are countless examples throughout the universe where things break down, deteriorate, and degrade over time. We know that metals rust, we get old, and something just always seems to go wrong and break down. Eventually, even stars burn out. From a humorous perspective, we say if there is any law in the universe that should be repealed, it should be the law of entropy.

SYNTROPY IS AN IMPORTANT
GIFT FOR EMPOWERING LEADERS

We live in a polarized universe, where almost everything has an opposite. You can think of this as a bad news/good news story. The bad news is that there is entropy in the universe, and many things fall under its purview. So what's the good news? Well, the good news is that because we live in a world of opposites, there is a phenomenon you can think of as antientropy, or *syntropy*. Syntropy then stands for the propensity in the universe for things to get better and for systems to become more complex and more efficient and evolve in a positive direction. These phenomena have been observed in the natural world and also has implications, not only in our personal lives but in our organizations.

Scientists are still debating which force in the universe is stronger, entropy or syntropy. But here on earth, we know that things left alone will begin to deteriorate. Entropy moves very slowly unless there is some external action or intervention. You need a proactive intervention to stop things from deteriorating. It's like turning the dial back the other way. That's where leadership comes in. Leadership is about inserting yourself into the natural rhythm of things to change them for the good. Things don't fix themselves. It's our ability to intervene that makes the difference.

One of the keys to empowering leadership is to know how much intervention is required and how much things need to be left alone. Picture a street performer spinning a plate on a stick. Left alone, the plate will slow down; entropy will take over, and the plate will crash. If the intervention is too great, the plate is going to spin off because it's going too fast. The street artist has to intervene with the right touch to keep the plate spinning at the right speed. An empowering leader understands what the right touch looks like to keep that balance going so that entropy becomes syntropy. There is a skilled touch involved in empowering leadership that turns destructive processes into creative ones.

There's a concept from a branch of science called "chaos theory" that says our world is an interplay between chaos and order. A world that was totally ordered would be rigid, inflexible, and stifling. A world that was totally chaotic would be dysfunctional. We need the right balance between chaos and order. Entropy plays a role in moving things toward disorder, and syntropy plays a role in moving things in the direction of order and complexity. There is a dynamic interchange that is constantly in motion, which is like a never-ending dance. Our role as leaders is to orchestrate the process so that syntropy prevails.

Some leaders crash their systems into the wall because they intervene so dramatically and constantly that they don't allow the forces within the organization to find their own natural rhythms and their own ways forward. There are other leaders who are so removed from the process that they don't coach people when they need to be coached, and they don't modify direction when it needs to be modified. They don't provide the support or the right resources when it's necessary. There is a line between those two things where empowering leadership falls. Empowering leaders figure out how to utilize these natural rhythms to move things in a positive direction. The empowering leader continually looks for opportunities to tip the scale in favor of syntropy for their organization.

MAKING THE WORLD BETTER IS AN IMPORTANT VALUE FOR EMPOWERING LEADERS

Making the world better gives you a reason for being. As we said previously, there are two forces at work: the force of destruction—entropy; and the force of construction, creation, and bringing things together—syntropy. There is a constant choice at work in nature and in the lives of people. You have a choice. Empowering leaders choose the path of construction and creation. By its very nature, that makes the world a better place, and it's a reason for getting up in the morning. They try to make the world better for everyone, or certainly for those who are in their sphere of influence.

At times, the choices are very hard. On a trip to Prague, we met someone who had given up his job as a principal in a communist country because the communists wanted him to teach things that weren't true and not teach things that were. He had made a difficult choice, even at the cost of his livelihood.

On another trip coming back from Europe, we met a fireman from England who had raised $20,000 from a small village in England for the families of firefighters lost in New York on 9/11. We asked him why he had done it. He said, "Well, I had no choice." There are times, when operating from your core values and guided by your higher self, that you, as an empowering leader, really have no other choice but to lead in a way that makes the world better. Ostensibly, you can choose to move toward entropy or toward syntropy, but, if you're really an empowering leader, you can only choose one of those. The other choice isn't available to you.

Leaders should not be overwhelmed into thinking, "What am I going to do today that is going to have worldwide impact?" The notion of the world can be seen in countless ways. It means your department, your organization, your community, your state, and so on. We simply mean spheres of influence. Who knows where your ripples of influence lead? We live in an interconnected universe. At some level, what affects each part affects the whole.

Remember, *think globally and act locally*. Bite off a piece that you can chew and work on that. Don't try to do the whole thing in one fell swoop. Ask yourself, "What would be reasonable, within the constraints and the resources of my organization and the talents that I have?" In all likelihood, none of us can make a total difference in the world, but, we all can make *a* difference. Our cumulative effect will be total. As an empowering leader, keep this question in the background of your mind: "Is this making some aspect of the world better?" If this is one of your guiding core values, you'll know you're moving in the right direction. It doesn't take everybody to make the world better. It just takes enough to achieve a critical mass to trigger a tipping point.

EMPOWERING LEADERS MUST
COUNTER THE FORCE OF ENTROPY

Most organizations, even the good ones, left to the mercy of prevailing forces, will start to deteriorate over time. Empowering leaders have to keep their organizations from drifting, falling apart, and moving in the wrong direction. They have to stand up for what's right and work against the force of entropy.

We live in a dynamic world where virtually everything is continually changing. In an ever-changing environment, if you do nothing, you tend to go backward because the world is moving forward. This means leaders must continually take action just not to lose ground. As a leader, you have entropy, which is moving elements of your organization toward a state of disorder. But you also face the reality that the conditions that impact your organization are continually changing. Empowering leaders need to apply syntropic principles to counter the negative forces of entropy and to adjust to the dynamic changes that are always unfolding.

A story in Greek mythology captures this dynamic. Sisyphus was doomed to forever roll a rock up the hill. Each time he got it up to the top, it would roll back down to the bottom and he had to start over again. Even though the rock is always going to roll back down the hill (entropy), without a Sisyphus there to push it back up the hill (syntropy), you'll never have a chance to get it to the top. Empowering leadership is about getting it to the top. It's about conquering the hill, conquering the mountain, and overcoming the forces that may be working against your organization, your school system, or your company. Your role as the leader is to bring people together to work against the forces of entropy. It's a constant effort. You can't push the rock up part way and then decide to take a break, because the moment you step away, it's going to roll back. One of the frustrations of leadership is the constancy of the need for it. That's just the way it is. It's hard, constant, and necessary.

Of course, building on this metaphor of moving the rock up the hill, an empowering leader is going to attract other people to help him or her. You don't want a lot of people standing around watching you or sitting on top of the rock. Not only are you going to get a lot of people helping you, but you can organize them in shifts. Some people push it early in the day, and some late in the day, and some in the middle of the night, so you constantly have a fresh energy supply. You've got some people creating contingency plans. If the rock starts to fall back, perhaps you've created a little dip so it gets caught before it builds too much momentum. As a leader, you're trying to plan how far you can push the rock on any given day. You are also worrying about your people, keeping them strong enough and engaged in the process, and recruiting additional resources, making sure, if there is slippage, that the slippage is not going to be too severe.

As an empowering leader, you think of ways to counter the force of entropy. You may bring the workers water. You may stand on the side and chant "Yo ho ho ho!" to get the workers energized. You may put your shoulder to the rock along with the rest of the workers. You may go out ahead of workers to figure out which path up the hill is going to have the fewest impediments to allow the rock to roll up more smoothly. The role of leader is varied and changes over time. It is not a single-dimensional activity. It changes based on the support you have in your organization and the team you have put together. It changes according to the conditions at a particular point in time. Your job is going to be based upon the situation and on the team you are able to pull together. But it is always being proactive and intervening when needed.

FINDING ORDER AND OPPORTUNITY WITHIN CHAOS AND DISORDER

Knowing when to intervene depends on our ability to see underlying patterns and potential opportunities for order and growth in the midst of chaos and disorder.

In every circumstance there is the opportunity to bring something positive out of the negative, something good out of the bad. Our scientists have found that in the natural world, where there is vast randomness and unpredictability, there are also underlying patterns of order and predictability. Pockets of order seem to emerge out of chaos spontaneously. Once we realize that is the way the world is constructed, we can follow the lead of the universe itself and take advantage of it.

All leaders find themselves in chaotic situations. They find themselves in circumstances that are dysfunctional and disorderly. Empowering leaders know where to look to see the positive patterns within the chaos. Once you identify them, you can focus people's attention on them and marshal people's natural inclinations to want to do something good, to want to do something positive, to want to be effective, to want to make a difference. All those inherent qualities that people have need a rallying point, a focus. It is the empowering leader who is able to see that in the midst of darkness and chaos or what appears to be doom and gloom, there is a way forward.

Someone has to be hopeful and give others hope in the midst of the storm. Someone has to know that there is a rainbow lurking around. It may be partly psychological, but that person is you, the empowering leader. Despite the difficult situation, you can see the possibilities, because all the negative circumstances do in fact present positive possibilities for improvement. When you have a situation with weakness, chaos, or disorder, there is the potential for tremendous order and success. As an empowering leader, you have to know that this is true. Then you can capitalize on it and organize around it.

To some extent, everything is chaotic until you understand it. You can look at any situation through a set of eyes that doesn't understand what's going on and it will appear chaotic. Now, through a set of eyes that understands what's happening, it's not at all chaotic. The following story illustrates this point. When one of our colleagues visited Vietnam, for the first few days he couldn't figure out how to cross the street. What he saw looked like utter chaos with a constant flow of traffic, mostly motorcycles going by without any apparent rules or traffic lights. Then, a little kid showed him how to cross the street. You cross it by stepping out. You never cross the street by standing on the sidewalk. There's a little rule there. You can't get across to the other side until you step out. You have to step into the traffic. Once you did that, there were a whole set of social rules where people riding the motorcycles knew how to avoid running over you.

As a pedestrian, you had to walk at a constant speed. By walking at a constant speed, motorists could calibrate how fast you were going. Then they would go in front of you or behind you, but none of them would run over you. From one perspective, it looked like utter chaos. Once the rules were understood, it was almost like a dance—a ballet—where being part of the action created a feeling of euphoria.

Part of the leader's role is to help make sense for people out of the apparent chaos. Leaders have to try to find those inherent rules, to find the principles and values at work. The core values that we've identified that are at work in organizations and in our lives allow things to take place in a way that makes them orderly, productive, creative, and constructive. Your role as an empowering leader is to make sense of things and to help people see where the patterns are and to see where the order is within the chaos that people may be experiencing. The reality is that most of our lives appear chaotic most of the time to most of us. Yet there are many times where there is great insight and great understanding if we open our eyes to see it.

FOSTERING SYNTROPY WITHIN YOUR ORGANIZATION

Empowering leaders can help people in their organization understand the concepts of entropy and syntropy so that they can identify when each of these forces is prevailing and operating. They can help the people in the organization understand that they are part of the dynamics that determine whether entropy or syntropy is going to dominate in any given set of circumstances. Often, it is a choice. Leaders can encourage people to work cooperatively and collaboratively toward the common good and in a way that fosters growth, productivity, efficiency, happiness, and joy. Many of these things are under our control. We can influence them with our intention. We can influence them with the structures we create. We can influence them with our recognition systems, our reward systems, and our communication systems. These are all things that we can co-create in our organizations.

Empowering leaders help people to believe in themselves and in their capacities to do what needs to be done. They help people to believe in each other, and the worthiness each of them has to be supported by one another. One of the ways you create a sense of syntropy in your organization is by fostering a belief in each other and an understanding that we are all a part of bigger patterns and dynamic forces at work in the world, like entropy and syntropy.

As we get a deeper understanding of how the world works, we can marshal those forces to enhance life and create the common good. As empowering leaders, we can use our understanding of these scientific principles to say, "Alright. I'm going to apply these principles in such a way that's not only good for me but that's good for the world at large. When I'm using these scientific principles in alignment with the core values delineated in this book, I play a role in enhancing life itself."

BEING A "STRANGE ATTRACTOR"

The concept of the "strange attractor" comes from the field of chaos theory. Scientists studying chaotic, nonlinear systems observed that there were patterns embedded in chaotic systems. As they investigated further, it seemed as if there was a central point, a starting point, around which orderly patterns began to coalesce or evolve out of what was previously pure chaos. These patterns were self-organizing and would grow over time around a central attractor. The scientists couldn't explain exactly what that attractor was; only that it was there. Out of chaos, order emerged. Over time, the order grew to higher orders of organization and complexity, but at its core, there was always a strange attractor drawing everything needed together.

We think this is a great metaphor for empowering leadership. It is about being the force that draws what is needed to you. It is being in the midst of chaos and finding meaning in it. In some cases, the leaders can *be* the meaning. If their vision is clear and their goals are worthy and noble, they can create rationality amidst the chaos.

Think of someone like Winston Churchill, during WWII, who by the sheer force of his being, rallied a nation and gave his people reason to hope and fight. Mayor Giuliani, in a different way, played a similar role after 9/11. Clearly, in times of crisis and stress, empowering leaders are able to step forward and give people a sense of "This is what we are about. This is what we can do." You become the torch bearer that gets people through the chaos and the darkness; the spotlight that focuses the light on what needs to happen. You become the focal point around which people rally. You become the strange attractor.

There's another way to look at this phenomenon. You've heard expressions like, "I don't like his vibe." Or, "I just feel good when I'm around him or her." Or, "He lifts my spirits." Or, "He's always up." We talk about how others make us feel. On one hand, it could be what they say or how they say it. It could be what they do or how they do it. On the other hand, it may be something else entirely. It could a direct result of their energy field or *aura*.

We believe that all leaders function as strange attractors. Think of yourself like a magnet with a magnetic field. Not all magnets are equal. Some are stronger than others. Let's suppose you are an empowering leader who wants to become an even stronger empowering leader. Let's suppose you want to attract more and more people to your sphere of influence, thereby functioning as a more powerful strange attractor. We believe the more you embody the core values in this book into the fabric of your being, the more powerful you will become in attracting what you want and need to see your vision come to life.

As strange attractors, we attracted you to this book; now using syntropy and constructive action, we invite you to expand the circle of empowerment.

EMPOWERING LEADERS

- See syntropy as an important gift.
- Seek to make the world better.
- Understand how to counter the force of entropy.
- Look within chaos and disorder to find the opportunity for order.
- Look within chaos and disorder to find the opportunity for constructive action.
- Look for the opportunity to foster syntropy within their organization.
- See themselves as a strange attractor.

Afterword

We hope you found *The Empowering Leader* enlightening, engaging, and empowering. The following twelve core values are seeds of empowerment.

Using your unique gifts and talents
Manifesting your intention
Using affirmation
Having a sense of mission and purpose
Balancing head and heart
Manifesting your vision
Using visualization
Using expectation
Using intuition
Using awareness
Using your higher self
Using openness

As an empowering leader you will now be able to take advantage of the gifts of

Synchronicity
Syntropy

You might find it useful to sort these twelve values into three groups, focusing on one group at a time during each of the next three years. If you focus on each core value within the group for a three-month period, you could incorporate all of them into your style of leadership over a three-year timeframe. After every three months, reread the chapters you're focusing on, including the "to become a more empowering leader" section at the end of the chapter. Commit to putting the core value into action, formulate and carry through on a plan to do so, and watch what happens.

As you nurture these seeds of empowerment you will make better choices and increasingly become a more empowering leader—a leader with supercharged leadership skills.

We have formed a center that serves as an information network, a support network, and a forum for collaboration and training for people who are striving to become more empowering leaders.

Share your experiences with us at www.cfel.org. Sign up for our biannual e-newsletter/journal, *The Lens*. If you would like us to conduct seminars or training for you or your staff in the practice of these core values you can reach us at the email addresses below. Supercharged leadership is the path to a better and brighter future for us all.

Sincerely,
Stephen L. Sokolow (SLsokolow@aol.com)
Paul D. Houston (phouston@eddsnet.com)

Selected Bibliography

Albom, Mitch. *Tuesdays with Morrie.* New York: Doubleday, 1997.

Bolman, Lee G., and Deal, Terrence E. *Leading with Soul.* San Francisco: Jossey-Bass, 1995.

Bronowski, Jacob. *The Ascent of Man.* Boston: Little, Brown, 1973.

Bruyere, Rosalyn L. *Wheels of Light.* New York: Fireside, 1989.

Campbell, Joseph. *The Power of Myth.* New York: Doubleday, 1988.

Chambers, Shirley. *Kabalistic Healing.* Los Angeles: Keats, 2000.

Chopra, Deepak. *Ageless Body, Timeless Mind.* New York: Crown, 1994.

Chopra, Deepak. *The Seven Spiritual Laws of Success.* San Rafael, CA: Amber-Allen, 1994.

Collins, Jim. *Good to Great.* New York: HarperCollins, 2001.

Covey, Stephen R. *Principle-Centered Leadership.* New York: Summit Books, 1990.

Crichton, Michael. *Travels.* New York: Ballantine, 1988.

Crum, Thomas F. *The Magic of Conflict.* New York: Simon & Schuster, 1987.

Dyer, Wayne W. *Real Magic.* New York: Harper, 1992.

Dyer, Wayne W. *Wisdom of the Ages.* New York: Avon Books, 1998.

Dyer, Wayne W. *There's a Spiritual Solution to Every Problem.* New York: HarperCollins, 2001.

Dyer, Wayne W. *The Power of Intention.* Carlsbad, CA: Hay House, 2004.

Farson, Richard. *Management of the Absurd.* New York: Simon & Schuster, 1996.

Ferguson, Marilyn. *The Aquarian Conspiracy.* Boston: Houghton Mifflin, 1980.

Fullan, Michael. *Leading in a Culture of Change.* San Francisco: Jossey-Bass, 2001.

Gawain, Shakti. *Creative Visualization.* New York: MJF Books, 1978.

Gladwell, Malcolm. *Blink.* New York: Little, Brown, 2005.

Gleick, James. *Chaos.* New York: Penguin, 1987.

Greene, Brian. *The Elegant Universe.* New York: W. W. Norton, 1999.

Hawking, Stephen. *The Universe in a Nutshell.* New York: Bantam Books, 2001.

Hawkins, David R. *Power vs. Force.* Carlsbad, CA: Hay House, 2002.

Heider, John. *The Tao of Leadership.* New York: Bantam Books, 1986.

Houston, Paul D., and Sokolow, Stephen L. *The Spiritual Dimension of Leadership.* Thousand Oaks, CA: Corwin Press, 2006.

Houston, Paul D., and Sokolow, Stephen L. *The Wise Leader.* Bloomington, IN: iUniverse, 2013.

Hoyle, John R. *Leadership and the Force of Love.* Thousand Oaks, CA: Sage, 2001.

Jackson, Phil. *Sacred Hoops.* New York: Hyperion, 1995.

Jaworski, Joseph. *Synchronicity: The Inner Path of Leadership.* San Francisco: Berrett-Koehler, 1996.

Kessler, Rachael. *The Soul of Education.* Alexandria, VA: Association for Supervision and Curriculum Development, 2000.

Lenz, Frederick. *Surfing the Himalayas.* New York: St. Martin's, 1995.

Lipton, Bruce. *The Biology of Belief.* Carlsbad, CA: Hay House, 2005.

Markova, Dawna. *The Smart Parenting Revolution.* New York: Random House, 2005.

Millman, Dan. *Way of the Peaceful Warrior.* Tiburon, CA: H. J. Kramer, 1980.

Millman, Dan. *The Life You Were Born to Live.* Tiburon, CA: H. J. Kramer, 1993.

Myss, Caroline. *Anatomy of the Spirit.* New York: Harmony, 1996.

Myss, Caroline. *Sacred Contracts.* New York: Random House, 2003.

Nouwen, Henri J. M. *The Return of the Prodigal Son.* New York: Doubleday, 1992.

Peck, M. Scott. *The Road Less Traveled.* New York: Simon & Schuster, 1978.

Peters, Thomas J., and Waterman, Robert H. *In Search of Excellence.* New York: Harper & Row, 1982.

Ponce, Charles. *Kabbalah.* Adyar, Chennai, India: Theosophical Publishing House, 1991.

Quinn, Daniel. *Ishmael.* New York: Bantam, 1995.

Redfield, James. *The Celestine Prophecy.* New York: Warner, 1993.

Redfield, James. *The Tenth Insight.* New York: Warner, 1996.

Redfield, James. *The Secret of Shambhala.* New York: Warner, 1999.

Remen, Rachel Naomi. *My Grandfather's Blessings.* New York: Riverhead Books, 2000.

Ruiz, Don Miguel. *The Four Agreements.* San Rafael, CA: Amber-Allen, 1997.

Schiller, Marjorie; Holland, Bea Mah; and Riley, Deanna, eds. *Appreciative Leaders: In the Eye of the Beholder.* Chagrin Falls, OH: Taos Institute, 2001.

Senge, Peter, et al. *Presence.* Cambridge, MA: Society for Organizational Learning, 2004.

Sharamon, Shalila, and Baginski, Bodo. *The Chakra Handbook.* Wilmot, WI: Lotus Light, 1991.

Simpson, Liz. *The Book of Chakra Healing.* New York: Sterling, 1999.

Thompson, Scott. *Leading from the Eye of the Storm.* Lanham, MD: Rowman & Littlefield Education, 2005.

Waitley, Denis. *Seeds of Greatness.* New York: Simon & Schuster, 1983.

Wheatley, Margaret J. *Leadership and the New Science.* San Francisco: Berrett-Koehler, 1992.

Wilkinson, Bruce. *The Prayer of Jabez.* Sisters, OR: Multnomah, 2000.

Zukav, Gary. *The Seat of the Soul.* New York: Fireside, 1989.

Zukav, Gary. *Soul Stories.* New York: Simon & Schuster, 2000.

About the Authors

Paul D. Houston, former executive director of the American Association of School Administrators, has established himself as one of the leading spokespersons for American education through his extensive speaking engagements, published articles, and his regular appearances on national radio and television. He is currently coauthoring a series of books on wise leadership and is president and a founding partner of the Center for Empowered Leadership.

Houston served schools in North Carolina, New Jersey, and Alabama prior to serving as superintendent of schools in Princeton, New Jersey; Tucson, Arizona; and Riverside, California.

Houston has also served in an adjunct capacity for the University of North Carolina, Harvard University, Brigham Young University, and Princeton University. He has served as a consultant and speaker throughout the United States and internationally, and he has published more than 150 articles in professional journals.

Houston completed his undergraduate degree at The Ohio State University, received his master's degree at the University of North Carolina, and earned a doctorate of education from Harvard University.

In 1991, Houston was honored for his leadership in urban education when he received the Richard R. Green Leadership Award from the Council of the Great City Schools. In 1997, he was awarded an honorary doctorate of education from Duquesne University. The Hope Foundation honored Houston with the Courageous Leadership Award of 2000. The Horace Mann League presented Houston with the league's 2001 Outstanding Educator Award, citing him as an articulate spokesperson for strong and effective public education. Houston coauthored the book *Exploding the Myths*, published in 1993, and in 1997 published *Articles of Faith & Hope for Public Education*. In 2004, he published *Perspectives on American Education*. Houston coauthored *The Spiritual Dimension of Leadership* in 2006 and *The Wise Leader: Doing the Right Things for the Right Reasons* (2013). In 2010, he authored *Giving Wings to Children's Dreams*.

Houston is committed to advocacy for public education and the children it serves.

Stephen L. Sokolow, a former superintendent of schools, is currently coauthoring a series of books on leadership. He is a founding partner and executive director of the Center for Empowered Leadership.

Sokolow served schools in Pennsylvania and Delaware prior to serving as superintendent of schools in the Upper Freehold Regional School District in Monmouth County, New Jersey, and the Bridgewater-Raritan Regional School District in Somerset County, New Jersey.

Sokolow completed his undergraduate degree and master's degree at Temple University, where he also earned a doctorate of education. He was awarded several fellowships and later served in Temple's Department of Educational Leadership as an adjunct professor. He is a past president of the Temple University Educational Administration Doctoral Alumni Association.

He is past president of the Superintendents' Roundtable in Monmouth County, New Jersey. From 1986 through 2001, he participated in the Harvard University summer invitational seminar for superintendents. Sokolow represented the superintendents of Somerset County, New Jersey, as a member of the New Jersey Association of School Administrators Executive Committee, and he served as a member of the New Jersey Governor's Task Force on Education.

In 1986, Sokolow was selected by *Executive Educator*, a publication of the National School Boards Association, as one of the top 100 small-district school executives in North America. He was honored for his leadership as a superintendent by the New Jersey Legislature in 1987 and was profiled by *The School*

Administrator, a national publication of the American Association of School Administrators, for his "out-of-the-box thinking" in January 1999.

His feature article on "Enlightened Leadership" was published in September 2002 in *The School Administrator*, as was his November 2005 article on "Nourishing Our Spirit as Leaders."

Sokolow coauthored *The Spiritual Dimension of Leadership* in 2006. In 2008, he was a contributor to *Spirituality in Educational Leadership* as part of the Soul of Educational Leadership series. Sokolow coauthored *The Wise Leader* in 2013.

Sokolow is a member of the clinical faculty at Seton Hall University where he conducts seminars on leadership and serves as a leadership coach for urban school leaders.

As a VISTAGE speaker, Sokolow conducts leadership development workshops for business leaders and CEOs.

Sokolow is a child-centered educator committed to empowering wise and enlightened leadership in both the public and private sectors, but especially in the field of education.